TEACHING ESSENTIALS

**Expecting the Most and Getting the Best
from Every Learner, K–8**

REGIE ROUTMAN

HEINEMANN
Portsmouth, NH

Heinemann

A division of Reed Elsevier Inc.

361 Hanover Street

Portsmouth, NH 03801–3912

www.heinemann.com

Offices and agents throughout the world

Library of Congress Cataloging-in-Publication Data

Routman, Regie.

   Teaching essentials : expecting the most and getting the best from
every learner, K–8 / Regie Routman.

     p. cm.

   Includes bibliographical references and index.

   ISBN-13: 978-0-325-01081-6

   ISBN-10: 0-325-01081-1

   1. Language arts (Elementary)—United States. 2. Effective
teaching—United States. 3. Teacher–student relationships—United
States. I. Title

LB1576.R7584 2008

372.1102—dc22   2007029448

Editor: Wendy Murray

Development editor: Alan Huisman

Production editor: Patricia Adams

Typesetter: Gina Poirier Design

Cover & interior designer: Lisa Fowler

Cover photograph: Dane Gregory Meyer

Manufacturing: Louise Richardson

Printed in the United States of America on acid-free paper

11   10   09   08   07   ML   1   2   3   4   5

For Frank

Contents

5. Embed Assessment **in All Teaching** 71

6. Teach for Independent, **Self-Directed Learners** 87

7. Put **Schoolwide Coaching** into Practice 113

8. Live a **Full Life** 127

A Note About Notes
and Other Resources

To keep the text clean and unencumbered, all references to research, ideas, authors, and quotations requiring explanation or further discussion are listed in a notes section beginning on page 132 in the end matter. The notes are divided by chapter and sequenced consecutively by page number. Sources and/or elaboration, including bibliographic information to help you find referenced material easily, are presented after a brief identifying phrase or statement linked to the text.

Any statement or concept not attributed is based on my own teacher-research, observations, and more than forty years of teaching experience.

In addition, practical, how-to support, video footage, and additional resources including a study guide are provided on the companion website, www.regieroutman.com.

Acknowledgments

I OWE A DEBT OF GRATITUDE TO SO MANY who have been unstintingly generous with ongoing help, feedback, and friendship. For the past decade, I have been demonstration teaching and coaching in schools and classrooms all over the United States, and, in Canada too. The joy of those residencies includes getting to know and learn from so many talented teachers, principals, and district leaders. All are esteemed colleagues; many have become treasured friends. The work we have done together, along with my teaching experience of forty years, is the foundation for the thinking behind this book. I am privileged and thankful to be able to share this collective knowledge and am grateful for the enthusiasm and energy that continue to infuse our collaborative work.

As I have always done as a writer, I depend on trusted readers to give me honest feedback. Darcy Ballentine, JoAnne Piccolo, Sandra Garcia, Marilyn Jerde, Thommie Piercy, Barbara Stallings, Terri S. Thompson, and Mary Yuhas read the entire manuscript and provided insightful comments and excellent suggestions, which are woven into this book and make it far richer. Special thanks to Richard Allington, Elizabeth Kappler, Cami Kostecki, Kaylene Johnson, Nancy McLean, Kathleen Poole, and Trena Spiers who applied their considerable expertise to thoughtfully respond to specific sections. And, thanks go to Rhett Johnson for his patience and skill in helping me improve my lagging technology skills.

Heinemann has been my publisher for twenty years, and I have great admiration and affection for the outstanding team with whom I work. I am especially thankful for my terrific editor and friend, Wendy Murray, a wordsmith who knows exactly when a phrase needs to be left alone or tinkered with. It has been a joy to work with her on this book and to benefit from her giftedness and gentleness. Alan Huisman is the magnificent development editor I depend on for total honesty and hard-hitting questions that push me to think harder and write smarter.

Lisa Fowler is the brilliant designer of all things big and small—the cover, interior design, and more. Abby Heim, extraordinary production supervisor, stays calm and efficient under pressure and masterfully coordinates all the pieces. Patty Adams, amazing production editor, leaves no detail unattended and beautifully formats every page, arranges each photo and chart, just so, and does it all with great efficiency, grace, and humor. Maura Sullivan, managing editor, adds her magic touch, sharp instincts, and gift for language in so many areas. I am grateful for her creative contributions and our special friendship. To the talented Kevin Carlson as well as Marla Berry, Nicole Russell, and Tom Meegan, grateful thanks for all your creative work in getting the *Teaching Essentials* website up and running. To Jillan Scahill and Karyn Morrison, thanks for doing all the behind-the-scenes work that kept everything humming along. Thanks, too, to Louise Richardson for ably handling the manufacturing, exceptional typesetter Gina Poirier, proofreader Cindy Black, and indexer John Brotzman. And to the educators and students of Ardmore Elementary School in Bellevue, WA, who opened their doors to us to take photographs for the cover and the inside pages, my deep appreciation.

Well before the ink on the book is dry, Pat Carls, director of marketing, brings her finely honed marketing skills to bear on getting the word out to the field. I so appreciate and admire all her capabilities and dedication—not to mention that she is literally willing to go the extra mile, flying to Chicago and Denver to meet me and see my residency work in action. Thanks, too, to talented Eric Chalek, Doria Turner, Kim Cahill, and the entire marketing team. I am so fortunate for all those at Heinemann who continue to effectively support my professional work in schools, workshops, and at conferences: Vicki Boyd, Buzz Rhodes, Cherie Bartlett, Angela Dion, Lori Lampert, Dusty Leigh, Maureen Foster, and Kristine Giunco.

Finally, President Lesa Scott and editorial director/vice-president Leigh Peake keep morale high and continue to take risks to ensure that new and important ideas, books, and products come to market. I have much affection and admiration for them both. To them and to the whole publishing team, I give heartfelt and appreciative thanks.

I feel lucky to be able to depend on cherished friends in my life. Harriet Cooper, best friend for forty-five years, always supports my efforts with much love and enthusiasm. The incredibly talented JoAnne Piccolo, Sandra Garcia, Marilyn Jerde, and Terri S. Thompson all deserve another mention. They have worked tirelessly with me in many different endeavors. For their brilliant thinking, bigheartedness and wonderful friendship,

I am most indebted. I am also grateful for dear colleagues and friends Claudia Mason, Judie Thelen, Jenifer Katahira, Lois Bridges, Diane Levin, Judy Wallis, Sheila Valencia, and Greta Salmi who continue to support my work and sustain our friendship.

Most of all, as always, I am grateful to Frank, my husband and soul mate, for his generosity, kindness, and lifelong love. And for Peter, Claudine, and our beautiful granddaughters, Katie and Brooke, I am so fortunate.

August 2007

A Brief History of a
Literacy Teacher, Learner, and Writer

TWENTY YEARS AGO, I began writing books for teachers as a way of sharing my teaching and learning experiences with the hope of improving instruction for *all* learners. Now, in *Teaching Essentials,* I share the culmination of forty years of teaching, coaching, questioning, researching, and collaborating. I describe what I consider to be the most essential practices and qualities of effective teaching and joyful learning. To keep this text spare, I illustrate the ideas and principles of the book on companion video-based, web resources, as there is almost no better way to show the how-to's of effective teaching than to allow others to see it via video footage taken in real classrooms. But before we begin this new journey, it is important to summarize the teaching and writing experiences that have led to this new endeavor.

My Beginning

I began writing with *Transitions: From Literature to Literacy* (1988), which describes learning in a school of mostly low-income African American students where about 50 percent of the students were failing to learn to read by the end of first grade. Many of these children had limited prereading experiences at home and very limited exposure to books outside school. Most did not know popular fairy tales, nursery rhymes, and children's books. I wrote a proposal to replace the commercial basal reading texts and worksheets and instead flood a first-grade classroom with wonderful children's literature and use that literature along with daily writing to teach reading.

"As a teacher-researcher, when I explicitly taught reading and its component skills using the best of children's literature, my students not only learned to read, they learned to enjoy reading and to choose to read."

We introduced daily journal writing and published children's written stories, both fictional and autobiographical, and discovered it was a powerful way into reading and into teaching and assessing phonics and phonemic awareness (although that term wasn't in our vocabulary then). We began a schoolwide publishing program that distributed these stories, turning children into esteemed authors. We showed that it was possible for all students to learn to read and write regardless of their language, culture, or background. Teachers and students read, reread, discussed—and sometimes sang and chanted—between six and ten texts each day.

It was the mid-1980s and I was on fire for what might be possible for students who deserved more than they were getting. The first enlarged-text books (later dubbed Big Books) were available in the United States for shared reading (that marvelous replication of the "bedtime story" environment from the home to the classroom), the invention by the brilliant New Zealand educator, Don Holdaway. Reading these familiar texts over and over led us to innovate on the patterns and storylines with our own stories, which we often wrote as oversized texts, and these renditions became favorite reading texts for the classroom.

I read everything in the professional literature that I could lay my hands on. I began subscribing to *The Reading Teacher* and *Language Arts*. I attended my first International Reading Association conference. I devoured books to feed my hunger to learn everything I could about literacy. I discovered the work of Donald Graves, Kenneth Goodman, Delores Durkin, Gordon Wells, Nancie Atwell, Lucy Calkins, Margaret Meeks, Connie Weaver, Frank Smith, Jan Turbill, Andrea Butler, Brian Cambourne, Marie Clay, Richard Gentry, and many others.

As a reading specialist working with "skill and drill" in thirty-minute pull-out segments, I did not see my struggling students making lasting improvements in either their reading or their self-confidence. As a teacher-researcher, when I explicitly taught reading and its component skills using the best of children's literature, my students not only learned to read, they learned to enjoy reading and to choose to read. I knew I was on to something. *Transitions*, originally published in Australia and later published by Heinemann, was the first book by an American teacher that detailed the use of high-quality predictable books (that I had also leveled) to teach reading, and it found a wide audience.

I was amazed by the power of the written word. I had not known until then the far-reaching influence that was possible through writing. I received letters from many teachers—telling me their stories, asking questions, urging me to go on writing. I continued full-time teaching. I read extensively, studied what I read, and considered the research. I became trained as a Reading Recovery teacher and finally felt competent as a teacher of reading. I went on writing, for an audience of teachers just like me, wanting to do what's right and best for children and maintain sensible and sane practices in a test-obsessed culture, just like the culture today.

Eager to expand on my beliefs about language learning, I wrote *Invitations: Changing as Teachers and Learners K–12* (1991, 1994), which described for teachers how to create a balanced literacy program that includes such elements as shared writing, writing in kindergarten, teaching phonics and spelling, responding to literature, teaching students with learning disabilities, meaningfully assessing and evaluating, and more. Believing that for teachers to be effective they have to be highly knowledgeable about current research, best practice, and excellent resources, I began including in my books for teachers my signature Blue Pages, extensive annotations of recommended professional resources and children's books that I wrote and periodically updated and expanded with the talented assistance of Susan Hepler and Judy Wallis.

Taking **a Stand**

In the mid-1990s, with the backlash against whole language rampant, I took a strong political stance and wrote a book for educators and parents, *Literacy at the Crossroads: Crucial Talk About Reading, Writing, and Other Teaching Dilemmas* (Routman, 1996). I researched and reported on the school bashing taking place in California and Texas and all across the country. I wrote with the conviction that we teachers must take a stand on critical literacy issues. The book gives suggestions on specific responsive action. It includes a chapter, "Phonics Phobia," that clarifies what research says about phonics and translates that research into sensible practice. I end the book with a section, "Empowerment for Life," which begins with a statement that still reflects my deepest beliefs today:

> I believe the ultimate in education is reached when learners—both students and teachers—take charge of their own learning and use their education to lead rich and satisfying lives. That is, as learners, they are able to inquire independently about everything that interests them, choose to read and write for their own purposes, find and use resources to seek the knowledge and information they desire, write to learn, reflect, think, modify their thinking, and take new action. Further, they constantly set goals for themselves, self-evaluate, seek feedback, and go on learning. Even very young children can do this—and they do, when teachers and other experts (such as parents and fellow students) serve as models and mentors. (p. 147)

I continued to teach and to learn everything I could to do the best teaching job possible. I attended professional conferences, read voraciously, and collaborated with colleagues. I subscribed to *Educational Leadership, Phi Delta Kappan, Reading Research Quarterly,* and *Education Week* to stay current with research and national issues related to literacy practices.

In 2000, I published *Conversations: Strategies for Teaching, Learning, and Evaluating* (Routman, 2000), my follow-up book to *Invitations*. I wanted teachers to have my growing body of knowledge and experience in one comprehensive book, and I hoped it would compel them to find their own voices through the power of conversation. Focused talk isn't just a perk of teaching and learning, but a necessity. Ongoing professional conversations among peers, student-led literature conversations, partner and small-group collaboration—these exchanges of ideas are at the heart of engagement and learning. Each chapter in *Conversations* is complete within itself so the book can be read in any order that suits the reader— on such topics as teacher as professional, teaching reading, teaching for strategies, spelling and word study, reading nonfiction, journal writing, organizing for writing, writing in multiple genres, curriculum inquiry, evaluation, and, of course, the extensive Blue Pages.

> *"Ongoing professional conversations among peers, student-led literature conversations, partner and small-group collaboration—these exchanges of ideas are at the heart of engagement and learning."*

In 2000 I also completed *Kids' Poems: Teaching Children to Love Writing Poetry* (four separate volumes—kindergarten, grade 1, grade 2, and grades 3–4). I developed the series because of the powerful way free verse poems freed up students to write with confidence and voice in a way no other writing form could equal. For me, the uniqueness and delight of these books are that the students' rough drafts with their invented spellings are shown side by side with their published poems, so readers see exactly how all kids—and teachers too—can easily experience immediate success and joy in writing.

Based on my continuing work in schools and classrooms, in 2003 I published *Reading Essentials: The Specifics You Need to Teach Reading Well* and, in 2005, its companion volume, *Writing Essentials: Raising Expectations and Results While Simplifying Teaching* (which also includes a DVD show-ing examples of effective and efficient conferences). I framed both texts with an Optimal Learning Model based on demonstrations, shared experi-ences, and guided and independent practice—phases of teaching that grad-ually release responsibility to the learner. I wanted to make life better for kids and teachers, to focus on what's most essential for high achievement, to delineate what effective teaching looks like and sounds like.

Knowing that the National Reading Panel report (on which the "No Child Left Behind" law is based) had rejected any consideration of the work of teacher-researchers like myself, I made sure that *Reading*

Essentials and *Writing Essentials* are supported by extensive research, both within the text and in a notes section at the end. Knowing, too, that teachers need explicit information, I included lesson plans along with discussion and demonstrations on such critical topics as bonding with students; teaching with a sense of urgency; teaching reading and writing effectively; emphasizing shared reading and shared writing; connecting reading with writing; teaching comprehension; teaching basic skills; ongoing evaluating through conferences, whole-class activities, and self-assessments; and, always, celebrating students' strengths.

Beginning Again

Every time I complete a book, I tell anyone within earshot that it is the last book I will ever write. I am exhausted. I have said everything I want to say. I want to have more time to live my life—to be with my husband Frank, our Peter and Claudine, and our granddaughters Katie and Brooke; to spend time with my dad; to be a good friend; to garden and cook and make jam; to read great literature (and the occasional lightweight guilty pleasure); to attend the theater and the ballet; to go dancing. And yet. I am a learner and a teacher. That is also my life. I continue to teach. Since 1997, I have been conducting weeklong teaching and coaching residencies all around the country. I put the Optimal Learning Model in use not just for students but for teachers—showing them how, teaching side by side with them, coaching them, teaching and demonstrating in their classrooms, raising expectations for what's possible, and attempting to bring the joy back into teaching and learning.

I remain highly conscious of the enormous pressure and stress teachers and administrators face. More and more is added to the curriculum, "training" for these new programs is often inadequate, and nothing is ever taken away from what teachers are required to do. I am passionate about making life easier and saner for teachers and students everywhere while at the same time increasing achievement and raising expectations for what is possible. Conducting my residencies, I continue to see little joy in reading or writing or teaching. It is that lack of joy and celebration, as much as any desire to improve teaching and learning, that compels me to go on teaching, writing, and speaking.

The work I am currently doing is the most exciting and challenging of my professional life. I am working with English language learners, special education students, struggling learners, and every manner of student and teacher in every kind of school, so I know what works and why it works

"When I am in classrooms, I am

both expert and learner.

I continue to ask questions, to try

out, to stumble, to seek new

answers, to rethink."

and what is truly essential for student success, high achievement, and worthwhile and lasting school change. After forty years of teaching, studying, and learning, I want to share what I know in my mind and my heart, through research and experience, through trial and error, through collaboration, through deep reflection, through plain hard work and persistence.

When I am in classrooms, I am both expert and learner. I continue to ask questions, to try out, to stumble, to seek new answers, to rethink. Each book I have written is new and is a reflection of where I am now in my thinking and learning. *Teaching Essentials* is a summation of beliefs, principles, and ideas about instruction and learning that apply to all grade levels and in all disciplines. It is my shortest book, and like my others it is plain spoken and easy to read out of respect for you, my esteemed reader, and your busy life. It is based on a lifetime of teaching, coaching, and learning.

Teaching Essentials is supported by a companion website (please see *Teaching Essentials* on www.regieroutman.com) that allows teachers to see good teaching in action, whether they are working on their own or with peers on improving their practice. The website also incudes a downloadable study guide to promote professional conversations. Use the study guide to examine and discuss teaching practices across the curriculum with the goal of raising achievement and enjoyment for both teachers and students.

I've also taken the principles of *Teaching Essentials* and brought them to life in long-term professional development programs. Based on my ongoing residency work in schools, **Regie Routman in Residence** is comprised of three DVD-based professional development (PD) programs with accompanying detailed guides. Each PD program is a yearlong, professional development model for improving schoolwide and districtwide achievement. The three *Transforming Our Teaching* projects—*Reading/Writing Connections, Writing for Audience and Purpose, Reading to Understand*—show daily teaching and coaching in schools where I am conducting residencies. I have learned that teachers and administrators learn more and are more apt to apply what they learn if, in addition to reading and discussing a professional text, they can also see and hear what effective teaching looks like and sounds like and—with support and planning—try out and apply what they are viewing, analyzing, discussing, and thinking about.

My hope is you will use *Teaching Essentials* as a catalyst for your thinking: that reading this text may affirm what you are doing as well as create a little dissonance that causes you to reflect on your teaching. This book is an invitation to think and talk more deeply about how to improve and sustain effective, daily literacy practices across all subject areas and throughout the school year so that all students and teachers reach the highest possible levels of learning, achievement, independence, and enjoyment.

TEACHING ESSENTIALS

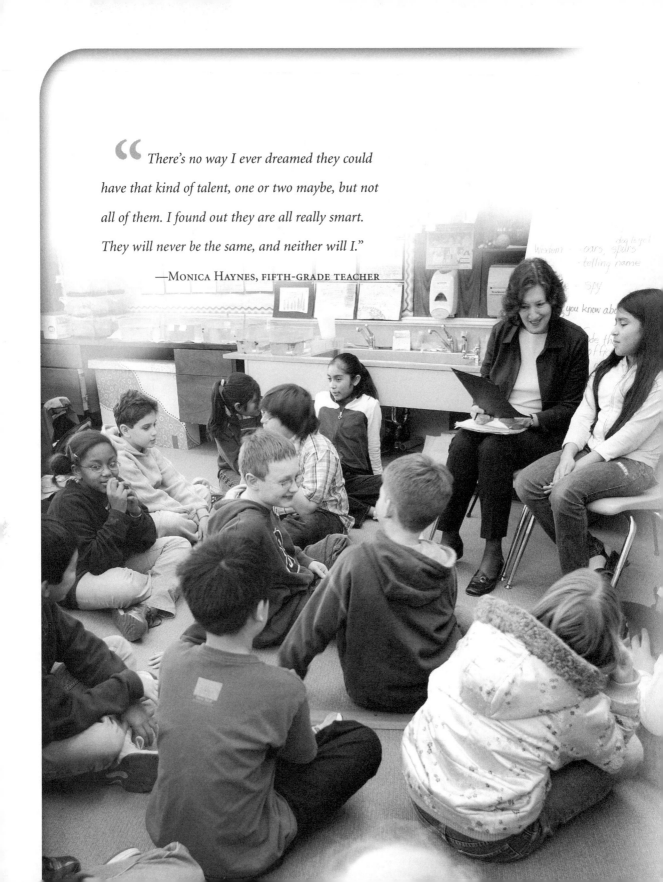

> *There's no way I ever dreamed they could have that kind of talent, one or two maybe, but not all of them. I found out they are all really smart. They will never be the same, and neither will I."*
>
> —MONICA HAYNES, FIFTH-GRADE TEACHER

CHAPTER 1

Look Beyond
What You See

I CAN STILL SEE THEM CLEARLY: two little girls, one black, one white, standing at the entrance to a first-grade classroom. What I didn't see then was how their teacher's narrow vision would permanently impact each child's life.

The white child and her mother were beautifully dressed, well spoken, and on time. The black child and her mother were more simply dressed, poorly spoken, and late. I watched unseen from my room next door as the teacher bent down and smiled at the white child and welcomed her into the classroom. When the black child arrived, the teacher looked annoyed, and hurriedly ushered the child inside. The child of color was already being treated as less capable. Her potential for academic success was determined by what was outwardly seen and perceived. The white child learned to read and moved on to second grade. The black child repeated first grade. Her future had been determined within moments of entering the classroom. That incident took place forty years ago, and little has changed. The biggest problem in education today is still the massive achievement gap between black and white children (*The New York Times*, 2007) and that disparity extends to most children of color.

> " *Teachers need to know that kids that look like they are not paying attention are the ones that are paying attention, and the ones that look like they are paying attention, sometimes, they are not paying attention.*"
>
> —KATHERINE, COLLEGE-BOUND EIGHTH-GRADE STUDENT, MISTAKENLY PLACED IN SPECIAL EDUCATION IN THIRD GRADE

We need to suspend our preconceived beliefs and judgment each time we meet a student, to assume that every child is capable. We must look beyond the physical impression—the dress, the language, the behavior—and believe all children of all cultures are talented. So many children are far more intelligent than they are given credit for. Every child has strengths; we just need to *see* them and begin our teaching there.

Invite **Everyone** into the Learning Community

When I conduct a residency, I insist that all children be included in the classroom—the special education students, the English language learners, and those with behavior problems—and that I not be told who the sup-posed "special" students are. Having no preconceptions, I treat them all as if they are smart, and amazing things can and do happen. The "yes, buts" disappear when people see the quality of what students can do, especially the struggling ones.

Here's an example. On my first day in a school where most of the students were English language learners from low-income families, I gath-ered the first graders together on the floor in front of me. Wanting to bond with the students and engage them quickly, I read aloud a storybook that I knew they would love, *We Love Saturdays y domingos,* by Alma Flor Ada. It's a charming tale about a child who visits his grandparents, the English-speaking ones on Saturday and the Spanish-speaking ones on

Sunday, and many Spanish words are sprinkled throughout. (We would later go on to write and read our own *We Love Saturdays* bilingual book.)

As I was reading, I noticed a little boy ambling about the classroom on his knees, seemingly not paying attention. I ignored his behavior until, from the back of the room, he burst out, "It's 'Abuelita,'" slowly stretching out the sounds of the word in his loudest voice and putting the accent exactly where it needed to be. I had a choice. I could either discipline him for perceived rude behavior or welcome him into the learning community.

"Cesar," I called to him. "Thank you so much for helping me with my Spanish. Now I know how to pronounce that word. Come up here and sit right next to me. My Spanish isn't very good. You can be my helper."

He did as I asked, correcting my Spanish as I continued reading the story. Each time he called out the pronunciation of a word, I acknowledged him: "Thank you for helping me learn Spanish and do a better job reading this story."

Can I say that Cesar's teachers never had another moment's trouble with him, that all his behavior problems disappeared? Not exactly. But here's what did happen. Cesar became part of the classroom instead of being further isolated. From the moment he was invited into the conversation, he listened eagerly to the story, and his teachers began to see potential they hadn't before. The truth was, as they later admitted, they had given up on him. He was not typically included in classroom language activities. As an ELL student who frequently exhibited off-task behavior, he was taught reading and writing outside the classroom.

When his teachers saw Cesar's attention, involvement, and alertness, they began to view him differently, to raise their expectations of his capabilities. In one week, midyear in first grade—through explicit instruction in a small guided reading group followed by much practice—he moved from reading level 1, where he had been stuck for months, to level 4. His first-grade teacher later told me, "By the end of the school year, I came to believe that Cesar was probably the smartest student in my classroom."

Once his first-grade teacher changed her vision of him, she took ownership for teaching him. She insisted he be included in all classroom language activities and expected much more from him in guided and independent reading as well as all subject areas. Cesar, used to getting attention by "acting out," slowly began to experience getting positive attention by being an active learner.

At the end of that weeklong residency, in our after-school professional conversation, Cesar's teacher made a profound pronouncement to the entire staff: "*You know, we all say that all kids can learn. But the truth of the matter is that the kids have to prove it to us first.*" How brave and

> *"When I conduct a residency, I insist that all students be included in the classroom—the special education children, the English language learners, and those with behavior problems—and that I not be told who the supposed 'special' students are."*

insightful of her to say out loud what most of us teachers privately believe and act on in our classrooms: it's only when we *see* what kids can do that we raise our expectations. We don't realize that we've got it backward. Once children enter the doors of our schools and classrooms, we have an obligation to ensure they reach their fullest potential. We need to see each child as capable right from the start. As soon as Cesar perceived that more was expected of him because he was smart, he began to work harder and become a reader and a learner.

Assume All Students Are Capable

Some years ago my dad had a brutal stroke. Nevertheless, he continued to improve cognitively for several years—largely because Frank and I have always held high expectations for him and talk to him on every occasion with the assumption that he is an intelligent man. It still rankles me when well-meaning aides, in a too-sweet voice, ask, "Manny, who is here to see you today?" then repeat the question—with more volume and less sweetness—when he doesn't respond. My dad doesn't respond because it's a pointless question. He knows who I am!

When I see my dad, I read him an editorial from *The New York Times*, tell him what's going on in the world, and treat him as the smart person he is. He is severely disabled physically but his mind is 90 percent intact, and he understands everything. We must do the same in the classroom—assume all students are smart and treat them that way.

When I met Kathy, she was a struggling, bilingual fifth grader. It was the third day of a reading residency, and I was demonstrating—for twenty or so observing educators, including the principal and the K–12 literacy director—how to conduct a one-on-one informal reading conference. (See *Reading Essentials*, pp. 100–110.) The teachers had deliberately selected Kathy to take part in this demonstration because she was one of the lowest-performing readers in the fifth grade. All I had been told about her was that she was reading at a second-grade level and that she was currently reading a book in the *Horrible Harry* series. I asked her to read a few pages of the book silently and was surprised that she was unable to say much about the story afterward. When I asked her to read a short passage aloud (in order to check her decoding and fluency), she stumbled over many words. Clearly this text and this series were too difficult for her. But how could I tell this reticent student, in full view of all the observing teachers, "This book is too hard for you"?

I had to make a decision, and fast. I thought back to Kathy's daily participation and engagement during our whole-class shared read-aloud

> *"She had been passed along, grade to grade, without the explicit reading intervention and instruction she so badly needed, and then as a last resort, placed in special education."*

of *When Marion Sang* by Pam Muñoz Ryan. I couldn't recall her ever raising her hand to volunteer a response during our interactive lesson, but I also knew she didn't stand out as a student who seemed confused. She had participated in "turn and talk," so I assumed she was capable and smart. I did not know she had been placed in special education and, therefore, would normally be excluded from a classroom reading lesson. I also didn't know she had been in this school since second grade and had not been taught how to read. She had been passed along, grade to grade, without the explicit reading intervention and instruction she so badly needed, and then as a last resort, placed in special education. Sadly, this is not an uncommon experience for many of our English language learners and other students who struggle mightily to learn to read.

I never lie to kids, so here's what I told Kathy:

> *I noticed this week as we were reading and discussing* When Marion Sang *that you seemed to understand the story. Am I right? [She nods.] Good, I thought so. You have a smart brain, Kathy. You have got the hardest part of reading and that's the understanding part, so I don't worry about students like you. What you're missing is the decoding part, how the sounds and words go together, and that's the easy part. We can teach you that.*
>
> *The book you're reading now is too hard for you because you're unable to tell me about the story. That's because all your energy is going into figuring out words, and there are many you can't read. That's not your fault. You haven't been taught that, and now we'll teach you.*
>
> *It means though, for a while, you will need to read easier books. If you keep on reading books that are too hard for you, you won't get better as a reader. We'll take you to the library today and help you choose a book that is "just right" for you. Are you okay with that? [She nods again.] You have a smart brain, Kathy. Don't forget that.*

Later, with the help of the school librarian, Kathy chose an easier book, *The Magic Finger* by Roald Dahl. The literacy director offered to teach Kathy the phonics skills she lacked.

Outwardly Kathy seemed fine with what had happened during our conference and the plans we made for her. But later that day I learned she had burst into tears after our conference and that the observing teachers were furious at me. How dare I come into their building and say one of their students hadn't been taught? These were kind and dedicated teachers, but they came to realize that no one had taken responsibility to teach this child to read.

Kids know when they can't read, and pretending it isn't so serves them very ill indeed. Saying out loud that the book was too hard was a relief to Kathy. Someone had finally said what she knew was true, and she

Kathy is now a stronger, more confident student.

didn't have to pretend anymore. To her classroom teacher's amazement, Kathy came to school the next day and told her, "I don't know why I feel so happy today, but I just do." We all immediately noticed her hand in the air for the first time, volunteering during whole-class shared read-aloud and giving smart, thoughtful responses. And after the defensiveness of the staff dissipated, there was a whole-school "takeover" to ensure Kathy became a reader. The staff also took a close look, grade by grade, at all students who were not competent readers. Then the grade-level teachers planned—with the leadership of the principal and the literacy director— how to intervene and teach those students.

Kathy received weekly support and mentoring in word work from the literacy director, read a large number of easy and "just right" books, and was held accountable for reading. Her reading progress and comprehension were closely monitored, and she quickly became a reader. In just five months she was reading long chapter books at the fifth-grade level. She had met her goal of wanting to be able to read like everyone else.

In March, two months after I met Kathy, her teacher wrote to me:

Kathy's progress is remarkable. Her entire attitude is upbeat and enthusiastic. The change in her has been incredible. Kathy is continuing to read books at her "just right" level, and is completing them at an alarming rate. Every Monday she can't wait to tell me all about the book she finished over the weekend. . . . I have seen growth in Kathy's confidence in all subject areas, as well as in social interactions. She volunteers daily in math, has a good group of friends, and is making good choices academically and socially.

In April Kathy wrote me a letter, excerpts of which are shown left. The excerpts reveal a newly confident learner well on her way to becoming a competent reader.

Far more difficult than teaching Kathy to read was removing her special education label. Research shows that when a language minority child is mistakenly placed in special education, it takes an average of six years to reverse this categorization. Only after Kathy moved out of state several years later did she, largely through her own advocacy, wrench herself free from her special education placement.

As an eighth grader, she wrote me and the literacy director at her former school a two-page, typed letter, talking about how smart she is, how she loves to read, of her determination to attend college, and about an upcoming trip she has been selected to go on "to see what college is all about." Some excerpts follow:

First of all, now I can read and I can also write. I love to read now. All my grades are good now, and now I get what the teachers are talking about. . . . I was one of the ones that never got attention and it was hard because I didn't learn anything. . . . Thanks to both of you, I'm such a strong girl and I know what I want and I don't let anyone stand in between me and school. . . . Well the last thing I want to say is never give up and follow your dreams and let my story touch your heart and make you want to do something with your life, and teachers never pick on kids because of their skin color or anything else and teach everyone the same way and pay them the same attention and never leave anyone out.

Wise words from a promising young woman. Kathy shows every indication of achieving her dream of becoming a lawyer or health care professional.

Value Diverse Languages and Cultures

Most of the schools that I conduct my teaching residencies in are multilingual and multicultural. It is not unusual for more than twenty languages to be spoken in a single building. I always view this diversity as positive; there is so much to learn and value from these fascinating students.

So I am taken aback when I meet teachers who see this diversity as a deficit and a burden. Yes, it's a challenge when kids don't know English and instruction has to be altered, but it's an exciting challenge. Students immediately pick up on whether or not we view them as capable. When we do, kids learn quickly; they teach one another. They seek to be part of the learning community. Of course, they still need lots of support, and much of this can be provided in the classroom with simple strategies such as:

- *Take dictation for kids who don't know enough sounds and letters to write.*

- *Seat students next to a classmate they like who can help them learn English.*

- *Schedule conferences at a time when parents can attend.*

- *Focus on oral language and storytelling.* Do what you can to ensure that students who need rich language experiences are not pulled out of the classroom during read-alouds, shared reading and writing, and other reading and writing activities.

- *Use language that is invitational.* I once asked an intermediate-grade student the genre of the book she was reading, which was about children who were imprisoned. She replied, "Realistic fiction," which on the surface seemed inappropriate. Suppressing my instinct to correct her, I said, "Tell me more about that." After she explained that members of her family had been in an internment camp, her reasoning made sense. Invitational language allows for divergent thinking and doesn't shut the child down. Statements like "say more about why you think that" or "I want to understand your thinking; tell me more" let our students know that what they think and say matters to us.

- *Celebrate your school's diversity and culture.* I walked into a school recently in which students came from many backgrounds, including Russian, Hmong, Hispanic, and Polish. I expected to see many indications of the pride the students took in these unique heritages, but the work displayed in the hallways had a homogenous look and feel. Take a look around your school. Make sure hallways and classrooms reflect an individual, heart-felt, creative environment, not a fill-in-the-blank one. This last point applies to all schools, diverse or not.

- *Select inspiring literature in which students see themselves.* One of the best measures of how we honor students' cultures and back-grounds is the breadth of literature we read aloud to them and make available in the classroom. Bilingual texts in particular allow English language learners to shine. If there are Hispanic, African American, or Asian students in the classroom, I make sure that these students encounter fictional characters that resemble them, that they can relate to the stories in the texts I read aloud and that we read together, and that similar books are available in the classroom library. If I can't find such stories, we write our own. Literature is one of the most powerful ways we educators can connect to our students.

"One of the best measures of how we honor students' cultures and backgrounds is the breadth of literature we read aloud to them and make available in the classroom."

Raise Your Expectations

I have *never* been in a classroom or school where the expectations are too high. In fact, I continue to be stunned at how little is expected from students. The greatest poverty I encounter in schools is the poverty of low expectations.

Low expectations exist not only in schools where students are primarily non-white and from families with low incomes. I encounter the same academic impoverishment in affluent schools. Often, high test scores—which are primarily due to the home literacy influence of highly educated parents—lull teachers into complacency and mediocrity. On more than one occasion, students have thanked me for the "gifted teaching."

Kids are kids. No matter where I teach and no matter the background, language, or culture of the students, I use the same challenging, engaging curriculum and strategies. I have worked in classrooms in which all the students are English language learners, and I teach them the same way I teach all children. I tell stories, find out what they're interested in, respect their language and culture, give them lots of opportunities to participate, make the curriculum relevant, explicitly demonstrate how to do what I am expecting of them, and provide lots of support through shared experiences, guided practice, and one-on-one conferences. I never talk down to them; I talk with them in much the same tone and diction that I use with adults.

Even students who are correctly placed in special education can surprise us. After spending a week observing me write poetry with a class of intermediate-grade students, a teacher applied what she learned with her special education students. A fifth grader with a reported IQ of about 50 wrote a short poem, "Candy" (see left). It's a great poem! Notice how well the title fits the poem, how rhythmic the words are, and how endearing the whole poem is. The student read that poem all over the school, to anyone who would listen to him. It was the most success he'd ever felt in school.

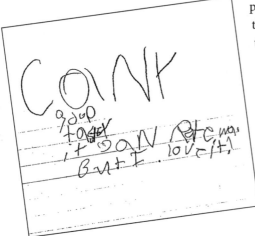

CANDY

good
tasty
it rots your teeth
But I love it!

Avoid Sympathy

I have worked with many well-meaning teachers who feel sorry for the complex and difficult lives their students lead. These teachers have caring relationships with their students, but they avoid pushing and nudging them toward excellence. "Poor baby," they tell me, "she has such a hard life." That may be true, but the best (and sometimes the only) hope we can give students for a promising future is an excellent education.

Without that first-rate education, many students will grow up and remain stuck in a cycle of poverty, low expectations, and limited opportunities. Sadly, in schools where many of the students come from families with low incomes, teachers settle for complacency and perpetuate mediocrity without realizing they are doing so.

Nothing bothers me more than seeing students shortchanged by well-intentioned teachers and administrators. It is not enough for us to work hard, teach the skills, and prepare students to take standardized tests. We have to work smarter and teach all kids how to learn so they can go on learning.

Aim High

Recently, I conducted a residency aimed at improving the teaching of writing in a metropolitan school in Denver. All of the students in the fifth-grade classroom in which I worked were low income and Hispanic. Most were writing at the third-grade level. Their teacher was devoted to her students and was working hard to help them achieve. But deep down she didn't really believe they could do grade-level work. Many of her students were English language learners; almost all of them struggled with writing, reading, and math. Neither they nor she looked beyond what they saw in front of them—a life of continuing struggle.

When we met to plan the week, she and the other intermediate-grade teachers requested I teach summary writing, in part because it was on the state writing test. I suggested we begin by teaching students how to write book reviews, which I find is an effective way for students to begin to learn about summary writing. Writing book reviews for a possible school website and/or local bookstores seemed like a good bet as a way to engage these reluctant writers.

The night before I was to begin teaching the students, I thought really hard about what I most wanted for them. It wasn't that they would learn to write book reviews. (That could come later.) It was that they would see themselves as writers, see possibilities for their lives, and see themselves as capable. Wouldn't writing for a more immediate audience and purpose engage them more fully? The next morning I suggested we change course and write about our dreams for the future and how we could realize those dreams.

We began by reading aloud to them, *Celia Cruz, Queen of Salsa*, the beautiful picture book by Veronica Chambers, illustrated by Julie Maren (Chambers and Maren, 2005) that tells the story of the famous Cuban Salsa singer. I wanted to inspire the students with this true story of how a child, just like them, found her way out of poverty and, through many years of study and hard work, realized her greatest dream.

I then wrote aloud in front of these students about my dream of wanting to replicate my residency work in many schools, not just the seven or eight I could presently manage to visit each year. My greatest dream was to make life better for all students and teachers, to create a professional development program that would be implemented schoolwide and districtwide, that would be yearlong, self-sustaining, and applicable across the curriculum. It would be based on my residency teaching in classrooms and explicitly show, on video DVDs, what effective teaching looks like and sounds like and how it raises achievement and enjoyment for teachers and students everywhere. My fear was I wouldn't be able to do it, that I was in

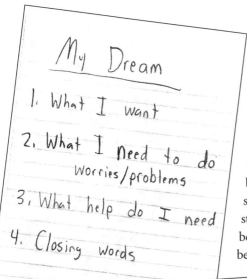

My Dream

1. What I want

2. What I need to do
   Worries/problems

3. What help do I need

4. Closing words

To Cherished Students

In just a few days
You captured my heart

Your kindness
Your honesty
Your stories

In just a few days
You broke my heart

Your worries
Your doubts
Your sadness

In just a few days
You changed my life

Your courage
Your hopes
Your determination

In just a few days
I hope you learned

You are capable
You are writers
You are smart

Hold onto your dreams
Don't give up
You can do it!

I believe in you.

From Regie Routman
With affection and admiration
November 9, 2006

over my head, that it would be too much work, that I didn't know enough to pull it off. I wrote about my dream, my fears, and the support I would need if my dream were to become reality.

I poured my heart out on a topic that was and is important to me. If I expected heartfelt, meaningful stories from the students, I needed to share an authentic one of my own. It is our own vulnerability and honesty in our storytelling and demonstration writing that helps kids feel safe to take a risk when they write. They also need to feel that we value them and their diverse cultures and backgrounds by sharing pieces of our own. Many teachers are afraid to get too personal with their students and then wonder why they get superficial stories in response to their prompts. It's a delicate balance. You want to be open and authentic with kids about your real thoughts, feelings, and beliefs without sharing inappropriate personal stories.

After I wrote my draft in front of them, I had students tell and write their stories. As preparation for writing, with gentle questioning, I first had several public conversations with students. We created a simple rubric based on my writing (see top left) that made it easy for them to organize their thoughts into paragraphs. We talked about making the audience the person who would be most likely to provide the support needed for the dream to become a reality.

In ten years of teaching in schools across the country, I have never before been so moved by a group of students. They poured out their hearts and their hopes and their dreams. They wanted to be doctors and lawyers, musicians, and inventors. They wanted to go to college but were worried they couldn't read and write well enough to qualify and wouldn't have enough money. They wanted to help their families get immigration papers so they wouldn't live in fear of family members being sent back to Mexico. They asked nothing of material value for themselves. They simply wanted better lives for their families, and at ten and eleven years old, they had pretty much given up hope that this was possible. Heartbroken by that sense of hopelessness, I wrote the poem (see left) and gave each student a personally inscribed and signed copy.

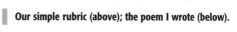

Our simple rubric (above); the poem I wrote (below).

Since the immigration issue loomed large for these students, we wrote a letter as a class (see below) and sent it to the U.S. Department of Education and the governor of Colorado, with copies of the students' "dreams" letters attached. When the children received thoughtful replies from the Secretary of Education at the Department of Education, the U. S. Citizenship and Immigration Services at the Department of Homeland Security, and Bill Ritter, the newly elected governor of Colorado, they were

Here is the class draft we wrote to send to the governor. Our finished letter got an amazing response.

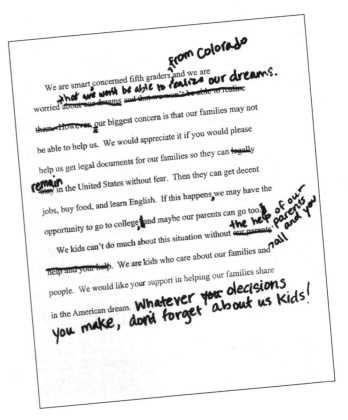

We are smart concerned fifth graders ~~and we are~~ *from Colorado* worried ~~about our dreams~~ *that we want be able to realize our dreams.* ~~and that we won't be able to realize them. However,~~ our biggest concern is that our families may not be able to help us. We would appreciate it if you would please help us get legal documents for our families so they can ~~legally~~ *remain* ~~stay~~ in the United States without fear. Then they can get decent jobs, buy food, and learn English. If this happens, we may have the opportunity to go to college, and maybe our parents can go too. We kids can't do much about this situation without ~~our parents', and your~~ *the help of our parents, and you* ~~help and your help.~~ We are kids who care about our families and *all* people. We would like your support in helping our families share in the American dream. *Whatever your decisions you make, don't forget about us kids!*

stunned and elated that their concerns had been taken seriously. Among the first words in their joyous letter to me were, "Our dreams were heard!" The governor concluded his letter to the students by stating: "I want to govern in a state where all the voices are heard, including those of our children."

The school district's director of elementary education and superintendent of schools also made sure the children's voices were heard. *Dreams: Listen to Our Stories* was published in an exquisite hardbound edition (shown on the following page) and distributed to policymakers across the state and the nation. The children and their teacher will never

A German student reading his dream story.

be the same. They see a future that is far beyond what they originally envisioned, and they are working hard—and succeeding—at beginning to make their dreams come true.

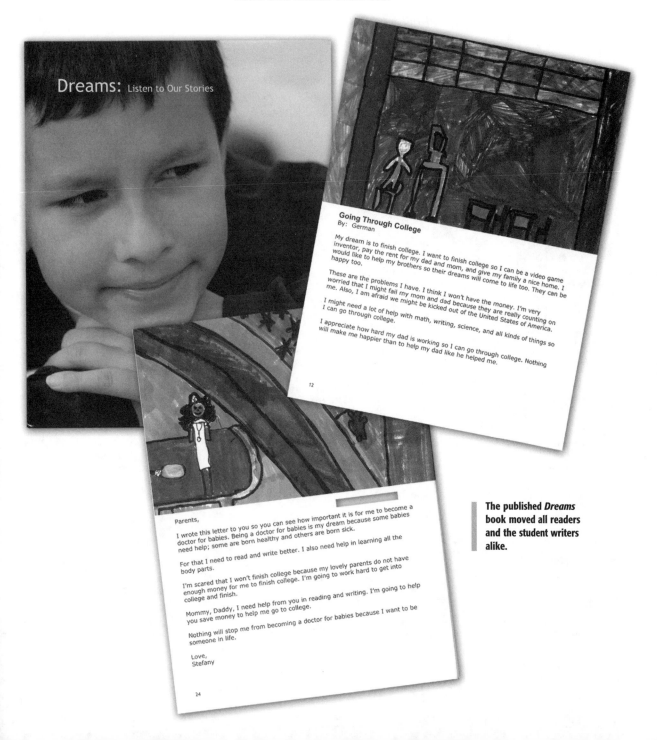

Dreams: Listen to Our Stories

Going Through College
By: German

My dream is to finish college. I want to finish college so I can be a video game inventor, pay the rent for my dad and mom, and give my family a nice home. I would like to help my brothers so their dreams will come to life too. They can be happy too.

These are the problems I have. I think I won't have the money. I'm very worried that I might fail my mom and dad because they are really counting on me. Also, I am afraid we might be kicked out of the United States of America.

I might need a lot of help with math, writing, science, and all kinds of things so I can go through college.

I appreciate how hard my dad is working so I can go through college. Nothing will make me happier than to help my dad like he helped me.

12

Parents,

I wrote this letter to you so you can see how important it is for me to become a doctor for babies. Being a doctor for babies is my dream because some babies need help; some are born healthy and others are born sick.

For that I need to read and write better. I also need help in learning all the body parts.

I'm scared that I won't finish college because my lovely parents do not have enough money for me to finish college. I'm going to work hard to get into college and finish.

Mommy, Daddy, I need help from you in reading and writing. I'm going to help you save money to help me go to college.

Nothing will stop me from becoming a doctor for babies because I want to be someone in life.

Love,
Stefany

24

The published *Dreams* book moved all readers and the student writers alike.

"*...wait until you see my writing! Come on. I want to show you....*"

—ALEX, A YOUNG WRITER

CHAPTER 2

Create an "I Can Do It!" Learning Environment

SUCCESS STORIES ABOUT STUDENTS WHO HAVE broken the cycle of failure have convinced me that once students believe "I can do it!" anything is possible. Again and again, I have seen remarkable changes in students once they achieve something they previously thought impossible. That triumph changes everything.

> *I can do it rised up. I can't do it went to its grave."*
> —OWEN, A THIRD GRADER ON BECOMING A WRITER

In *Writing Essentials* (2005), I tell the story of Owen, whom I met during a weeklong writing residency. From the time Owen entered school, he experienced great difficulty academically and behaviorally. In kindergarten, his teacher recommended him for special education. Although his mother refused that placement, expectations for Owen remained extremely low, and, predictably, he produced little. For example, in first grade, his teacher only expected him to complete one-sentence "story starters."

So it was a huge surprise to the observing teachers when in mid-February during my residency, second grader Owen volunteered to tell his "Secrets of Second Graders" story aloud and then went on to write a complete story that included a beginning, middle, and end, as well as humor, a good lead, a satisfying conclusion, conversation, telling details, and interesting word choices. He had it all, all because I made no assumptions about what he couldn't do (I didn't know his history). I assumed he was just as capable as the child sitting next to him, and indeed he was, and is. I helped him tell his story first, scaffolded his ideas and conversation, encouraged him as he wrote independently, and then celebrated his success.

Owen was transformed as a learner forever. I know, because I've followed his progress from second grade through fifth grade. Not only has he continued to improve, he is a confident student who enjoys learning and who now achieves at or close to grade level in all curricular areas. (See the samples of his teacher's letter and his letter to me.) Owen's story is a cautionary one. Had he been placed in special education in kindergarten, his life would have been very different. When I interviewed Owen and his mother after Owen had completed third grade, she urged teachers not to label children or give up on them. (My website contains a video clip of this interview.)

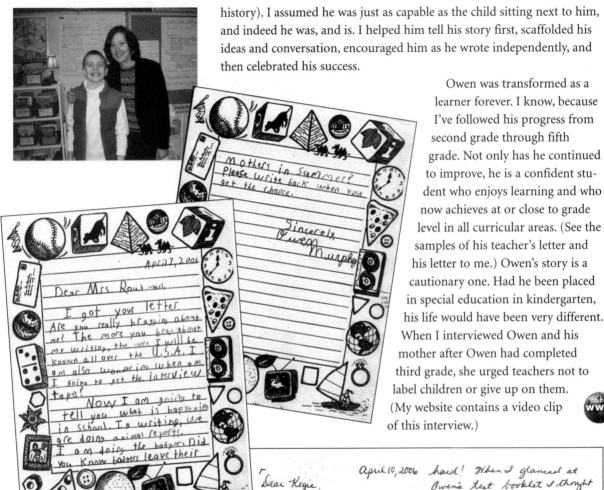

Here is Owen and his letter to me (see above), brimming with pride. His teacher's letter (right) confirms his amazing progress and the support he's received schoolwide.

Let Students Know:
"I Will Help You Discover the Possibilities"

It's five years ago. After my dad's brutal stroke he's had follow-up surgery to stop massive bleeding in his brain. He has tubes everywhere, is too sick to be placed in a nursing home, and needs the intensive care a combined rehab facility and hospital can provide. We arrange to have him flown by air ambulance from his long-time home of New York City to our new home city, Seattle, and he arrives depleted and depressed. His doctor tells us (to our dismay in front of him):

> *Your dad has had a very, very severe stroke, and it will take months and months for him to progress. It will be at least several months till the feeding tube can come out because his swallowing mechanism is so weak.*

Because of rules that don't make sense to us and that we don't understand, my dad can only stay at the current rehab facility for a month. Frank and I are frantic to find him a full-care facility. A nursing home seems our only option; yet he can't enter one if he still has the tracheotomy in his throat, which helps him breathe. We have not been told if or when that mechanism might come out.

Then we hear about the ventilators. Nationally, about seven out of ten people who are on a ventilator (a breathing device) never get off of it, but in this hospital, more than 70 percent of the patients have their ventilators permanently removed. The therapist who tells us this says that the hospital's patients on ventilators are all taken on weekly local outings—to the zoo, public market, parks, beaches, and so on. They see there is life outside the hospital, and that motivates them to work harder with the doctors and physical therapists.

We take that story to heart, and we instill hope. We tell my dad how important he is to our lives and that his grandchildren, especially, need him as a role model. We tell him that although he is physically disabled, his mind is fine and he can still have a good life. We promise to be there for him and make frequent visits a priority in our life. He works daily with the therapist, and the "trach" is removed in two weeks! His feeding tube comes out just a few weeks later.

I have no doubt it was seeing possibilities for his future that made him work so hard with his excellent therapists to achieve this positive result so quickly. It is the same with our students. We have to show them—through demonstrations, shared experiences, guided practice, helpful feedback, and ongoing assessment and encouragement—that, yes, they can be writers, readers, mathematicians, scientists, artists, chefs, dancers. They can be anything they want to be. We have to tell them—through our words, actions, and attitudes—"I will help you discover the possibilities."

Ensure That **All Voices** Are Heard

Everywhere I teach, I find that students' voices have been silenced. There has been no conspiracy or plan: it happens because we teachers do most of the talking and because we fail to recognize the importance of each student's voice being heard and the value of deliberated talk for deep thinking and learning. When students speak so softly that we cannot hear them, it is often because they don't believe they have anything worthwhile to say.

When I call on second grader Desiree after a turn-and-talk during an interactive read-aloud (see page 66), her voice is a whisper. Even with encouragement, she will not speak louder. I try hard not to repeat what students say (it sends the message that they don't need to listen to their peers), but today it is necessary. I make it a priority to get her voice into the classroom conversation, and each day her voice grows louder and more confident. By the end of the week, we can hear her. She is smiling more and stopping to hug me each day before I leave. (See Desiree's evaluation of her learning in Chapter 4, p. 69.)

We teachers need to set up and structure our learning environment to encourage participation that supports students' approximations and responses. Turn-and-talk shared writing, scribing responses in small-group work, self-directed literature conversations, collaborative group work, and shared writing experiences are all great ways to promote students' voices and thinking so all are heard and valued.

Act and Speak Respectfully

Treating students respectfully is an obligation, an unspoken pledge we take when we become teachers. I am therefore surprised whenever teachers comment: "You were respectful to every student. You didn't raise your voice. You were firm but you were kind and encouraging." Our students deserve no less.

"Our students discern whether or not we think they are capable and are advocating for them. They and we learn best in an environment where it is safe to take a risk and make a mistake."

The words we use, our tone of voice, and our body language speak volumes about our true attitudes toward our students, their families, and our colleagues. Our students discern whether or not we think they are capable and are advocating for them. They and we learn best in an environment where it is safe to take a risk and make a mistake.

Nobody is disrespectful to kids because she or he believes it's the right way to treat them. We get stressed out, have a bad day, or feel overworked and tired. Staff members need to support one another by being careful about the way we talk about kids among ourselves. We need to make it a habit to avoid negative talk about students in the staff room or team meetings. Negative talk and feelings can carry over into the classroom. Showing respect is a worthy effort. Our students can't learn well without it.

One of the first things I do after I meet a new group of students is consciously work on pronouncing each student's name correctly. It is a sign of respect every person deserves. Because all the students are new to me, I have each child wear a nametag bearing his or her first name. I tell them, "I always want to call you by your correct name. Names are important, and if I mispronounce your name, please tell me right away, so I get it right."

How we speak to and about our colleagues also lets them know whether we value them. My best advice is simple: speak and act exactly the way you expect people you love and respect to speak to you and members of your family—with kindness and caring and in a nonjudgmental manner. A positive tone conveys to students and to fellow teachers, "I respect who you are. I will do everything I can to support you."

Demonstrate the Power of Writing

Teachers are often surprised to see their low-performing students find their voices and confidence through writing. Once we tap into a child's interests and provide the necessary demonstrations and support to help him write, success can come quickly. I've seen a child change before my eyes in demeanor, facial expression, eye contact, voice level, and posture, once he is genuinely celebrated for his writing. The child looks different because he feels different; he is now a writer. Even when a child has experienced years of failure, it is still possible to break that pattern—especially by focusing on a writing topic that matters to the child.

I've thought a lot about why writing has the power to transform a child in a way I've rarely seen happen with reading. I think it's because in

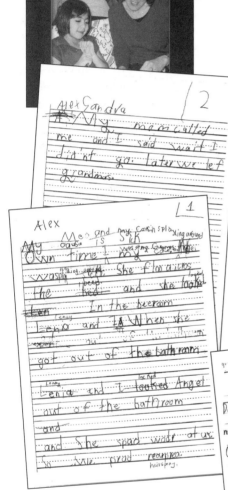

reading the book acts as a mediator: the words are already on the page and give the reader some support. In writing, the student confronts a blank screen or page and has to create the entire text, which is far scarier for many kids. So the triumph in writing, when it comes, is 100% the child's; the entire creation has come from the writer's hard won efforts. And for many students, writing success comes quickly, often faster than reading success does. With excellent teaching and a focus on the writer first and the writing second, a student can sometimes make the leap into writing in a single day. The child, initially downtrodden and unconfident, begins to view himself as capable, and that capability gradually extends to other areas. Owen's story (pp. 17–18) is one example of this transformation. AlexSandra's is another.

AlexSandra is the second-grade student on the cover of *Writing Essentials* (Routman, 2005). She is also featured in the writing conference on the accompanying DVD. The conference shows a shy English language learner who is struggling hard, even with much support, to tell and write an organized, meaningful story.

Two years later at a subsequent writing residency in her school, an exuberant AlexSandra flags me down in the hallway: "Mrs. Routman, wait until you see my writing! Come on. I want to show you, and I also want us to take a picture together." After two years of excellent teaching and meaningful daily writing, Alex's writing looks like any other competent fourth grader's. Alex beams with an "I can do it!" spirit.

AlexSandra, once struggling, is now an accomplished fourth grader.

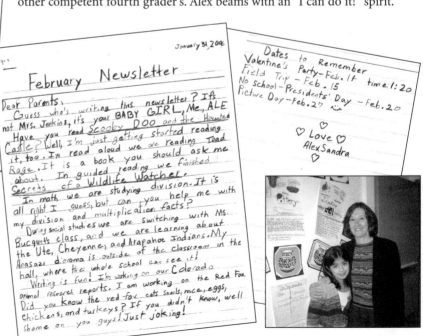

Do More Writing for Valued Audiences and Purposes

In a fourth-grade classroom in which the students saw writing as a "school thing" and typical writing samples looked like second-grade work, students were stunned when I told them the persuasive letters they were about to write would be mailed. "You mean we're really going to actually send these, put stamps on them and mail them?" several asked. Sadly, my experience has been that too often students view writing assignments as either "for the teacher" or "for the bulletin board."

I described the long persuasive letter I had just written to a Seattle hospital detailing the positive aspects of my father's recent stay and then also focusing on the many things that went seriously wrong and caused my dad to suffer needlessly. I provided specific recommendations for improving services for all patients and sent copies of my letter to patient care and specific doctors and nurses. I told students about the two letters I received back in return, the first a prompt reply from the chief operating officer and the chief medical doctor, thanking me for my letter and telling me an investigation of what I had reported would take place. Finally, I showed them the follow-up three-page letter telling me the specific changes the hospital was putting in place. I let students know that carefully written letters, positively worded, are taken seriously. Who did they want to persuade so that a practice or policy might be changed?

After much discussion, it became clear that most students were upset about a kickball rule on the playground during morning and lunch recess. Miss Vicky, the playground supervisor, whom the children liked and respected, had established a one-out rule that they wanted changed to three outs. All students had an opportunity to revise the letter with a partner or small group, which gave each of them a voice and also gave us teachers a record of their work and thinking. After a brief whole-class discussion with input from each group, the letter was revised and hand-delivered to Miss Vicky. (The shared writing draft, revision work, and final letter are shown on the next page.)

Miss Vicky came into the room a short time later and, with a smile, thanked the students for their letter, which she had in her hand. She explained in detail why the three-out rule would not work. I was expecting her to be impressed with the children's carefully worded, polite letter and at least offer to try out their suggestion. The room went silent. Not one student, not one of the many observing teachers, nor the principal (who was also observing) said anything. I was stunned by those silenced voices. Miss Vicky was about to leave the room.

"Kids," I said, "your whole life you're going to have people telling you what you can't do. If you just give up, you'll never accomplish your dreams. You were all pretty passionate about why you wanted that one-out rule changed. Tell Miss Vicky how you feel." Slowly, the students came to life. They began to speak in turn, very quietly at first. To each, Miss Vicky responded with a reason

the change wouldn't work. Her seeming inflexibility surprised me, but I encouraged the students to keep speaking their minds. Finally, one young man offered, "How about if we keep the one-out rule during our short morning recess but try the three-outs rule during the longer lunch recess?" I thought to myself, "This guy has a future as a mediator or a lawyer." And Miss Vicky said, "Now that's an idea we could try." The children were elated.

True to her word, Miss Vicky tried out the children's suggestion and found it worked. In her letter back to them, she followed their format,

Our shared writing draft, small-group revisions, and final letter showed the importance of writing for a purpose.

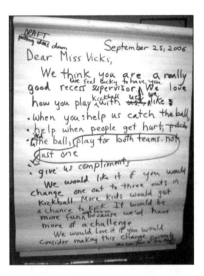

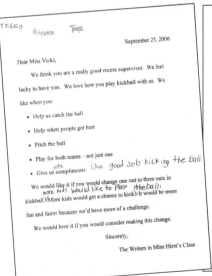

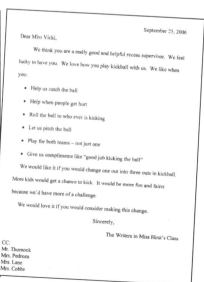

October 3, 2006

Dear Writers in Ms. Hirst's Class,

Both Miss Cecelia and I (Playground Supervisors) are lucky to have such great students on the playground. We both feel that all of you:

- play with safety in mind
- are respectful towards each other
- are helpful when new students are learning the game
- follow the rules of the playground

You are wonderful students to have a great interest in how we should play kickball. I am glad that a sport we play at recess time can make all of you come together and write a letter to better the game.

Now when you asked if we can change the one (1) out rule to three (3) outs, we all decided that we would try it for a few days. We did and it was a SUCCESS!! Both 4ᵗʰ and 5ᵗʰ grade groups will be playing with one (1) out on the 10 minute recess. We will play with three (3) outs on the lunch recess. Great job!

Thank you again for writing your letter!

Sincerely,

Ms. Vicky and Ms. Cecelia
Playground Supervisors

Cc:
Mr. Thornock
Ms. Pedroza
Mrs. Lane
Mrs. Cobbs

first positively stating the qualities she likes about them—using bullets, just as they had—before addressing the main issue. At the bottom left, she copied her letter to others, just as the students had done.

When the students went on to write persuasive letters—to family members, businesses, teachers, and so on—they took the task seriously, energized by the realization that their letter had the possibility of garnering the desired effect. They willingly revised and edited, and many of them did their best writing to date.

I believe that effective teaching is about hearing all the voices—making sure that every student is valued, heard, and respected and knows that his or her voice can make a difference. Many students have no idea about the power of the written word. Once they experience it, their lives are forever changed. This phenomenon is equally true in schools where most students come from families of affluence. Often I have found that high test scores coexist with scant student interest in writing, low engagement, and little understanding of audience and purpose.

Here's a typical story. When I've asked students to write to a family member at holiday time (as a gift to the person) recalling a special time with the mom or dad or requesting something (that doesn't cost money), many from families of affluence ask for more time with mom or dad—a request I've rarely seen from children of low-income families. This emotional impoverishment is as heartbreaking as any other poverty I encounter in schools; I have learned that all schools are "high needs" in different ways. The children who wrote the gift letters to their parents have every "thing" they could ever want, except the gift of time with a parent. When some of these earnest, carefully written letters got the desired effect, students—and some teachers, too—saw the power of writing, perhaps for the first time in their lives.

Use Writing as a Way into Reading

Midyear, in a kindergarten classroom where many of the students were second language learners and came from families with low incomes, we used writing as a way into reading: we used it to teach phonemic awareness, phonics, and word work; validate students' life stories; and create an "I can do it!" spirit.

Although the children had been doing some writing almost daily, that writing had focused primarily on letters and sounds and writing a structured sentence. Teachers had assumed that kindergarten kids first needed to know just about all their letters and sounds before they could be expected to write stories (an assumption they later revised). When I told my story about our cat Norman and how my husband Frank liked to feed her fancy tuna fish, not just dry cat food, the children were emboldened by my simple, close-to-home topic, and eager to tell and write their own stories. I thought aloud and wrote that Norman story on chart paper with the students looking on, so kids could see how a writer thinks through ideas and chooses favorite details as they write a first draft. After demonstrations, scaffolded conversations to help students tell their stories in detail, and ample time spent writing together, conferring, and celebrating, students were able to write meaningful stories fairly independently. The teachers and the principal who were observing were amazed at what *all* the students were able to do, including the many students who spoke Spanish as their first language. By the end of the school year, just about every student had acquired phonemic awareness without a specialized phonemic awareness program. In fact, their scores on the "Hearing Sounds in Words" test (Clay, 2002) surpassed district averages.

These kindergarten students are writing independently.

Perhaps the biggest benefit came later. At the end of the school year, almost all these kindergartners, including the English language learners, were readers. This was a remarkable first! The classroom teacher, reading specialist, and principal credited the daily story writing—which required lots of reading and rereading of text plus lots of word work (slowly stretching out words while saying them aloud, hearing sounds in words, and applying letters to those sounds)—as the pivotal factor.

I've seen it again and again; it is writing that turns children into readers. Meaningful word work based on students' own writing can then be easily integrated into the teaching of reading and writing. Here are just a few ways you can get the writing-to-reading connection flowing:

- Word-process (with correct conventions) a child's dictated or handwritten journal entries and turn them into a text.

- Take small-group shared writing pieces and read them first as a shared reading and then in guided and independent reading.

- Base literacy lessons on a class-authored text that has been read over and over again as a whole group and with a partner.

Particularly noteworthy is the dramatic impact writing, especially nonfiction writing, has on reading comprehension. I worked with Marlene Ellis for two successive years in her urban classroom, in which she taught the same group of students, as first graders and then again as second graders. At the beginning of grade 1, many of her students were struggling and could be considered "at-risk." At the end of second grade, students' scores on districtwide assessments indicated most were reading a year or more above grade level. By the beginning of third grade, many of these students were so engaged in school that, according to their teacher, "everyone was a star." Marlene credits the link between daily reading and writing (especially with a nonfiction emphasis), along with one hour of daily writing on topics they chose themselves, with these students' high reading comprehension and achievement. She comments, "I've noticed that with increased nonfiction writing, there's an increase in the desire to read nonfiction books."

Do More Shared Reading from Shared Writing Texts

Class-authored narratives based on experiences that are relevant to the students are always easiest for them to read. This is particularly true for English language learners, who need familiar language to experience reading success. I often take these common texts and use them in differentiated instruction. For example, in the primary grades, inspired by a great read-aloud book, we might write a class book titled "What We're Great At," "Our Favorite Colors," or "Classroom Procedures." While students each get a copy of the published text—which typically has only one, two, or three lines of text on each student-authored page—they also get to extend the page they wrote.

Many teachers also turn texts written by their students into Readers' Theatre scripts. The repeated reading increases students' reading fluency and word recognition, and performing the scripts for others increases their confidence as readers. An added benefit is that fluency is modeled and practiced in a natural rather than a contrived way.

First-graders read (and do more writing) for their class-authored nonfiction text on plants.

Read and Write Texts That Embody an "I Can Do It!" Spirit

"We need to do everything we can to show students what is possible—through the stories we tell, read, and write with them and through the literature we use to teach reading and other core subjects."

The statistics are staggering. Half our students in large cities fail to graduate from high school. Many of our young African American males are incarcerated. We have given up on a huge segment of society who have been made powerless in part through the failure of our educational system. We need to do everything we can to show students what is possible—through the stories we tell, read, and write with them and through the literature we use to teach reading and other core subjects.

In a third-grade classroom in which I was teaching students how to summarize and how to direct their own small-group literature conversations, I sought out excellent literature that would give these mostly economically poor Hispanic students hope and possibilities for the future. I did a shared read-aloud using the beautiful book *Rosa* by Nikki Giovanni (2005). Students heard and saw me think aloud and, with my guidance and scaffolding, had lots of opportunities to talk with one another and practice sharing their own thinking. Then heterogeneous groups of four or five signed up as a group to read, summarize, and discuss self-selected informational picture books about ordinary people who used extraordinary determination and hard work to make a big difference not only in their own lives but in the lives of others: Wilma Rudolph, Lou Gehrig, Celia Cruz, Caesar Chavez, Joe Louis, and others.

Similarly, in a fifth/sixth-grade classroom in a school where 85 percent of the students received a free or reduced-price lunch, we used the informational picture book *Sixteen Years in Sixteen Seconds: The Sammy Lee Story* by Paula Yoo (2005), about an ordinary Korean who achieved great fame as an Olympic swimming champion and became a role model for what's possible not just for Asian Americans but for all people who strive to overcome challenges and fulfill a dream.

Or again, in writing poetry in a sixth-grade classroom, a shared poem we composed on bullying, "No More Name Calling," served as a crucial text for showing students that writing could be used to change behavior. Students stated how upset they were about the bullying and name calling they had been experiencing since kindergarten. Students orally contributed ideas to the collaborative poem while the teacher scribed and guided the composition. The students chose to enlarge the finished poem, had every student sign it, and posted it in the classroom all year as the credo by which they would behave. Their classroom teacher said writing the poem was pivotal in convincing students they could make a difference.

Whenever I work in classrooms I bring a favorite book or two to read aloud to students and leave as a gift. Very often these are inspiring books in which the main character's "I can do it!" spirit leads to important changes and accomplishments. (See www.regieroutman.com for a bibliography of some of my favorite "I Can Do It!" titles.)

Celebrate

I always include celebration as part of teaching as a way to show students— and teachers too—what's possible. By celebration, I mean affirming, congratulating, showcasing, noticing, and making public the positive and specific actions and work learners have done or are attempting to do. In celebration, we focus on the learner's strengths.

Cheer Students On

Essentially, celebration means being a cheerleader. When I coach teachers after I have demonstrated in their classrooms and we have also tried some things out together (shared demonstrations), I tell their students:

> *Today your teacher will be doing all the teaching, and I will be her cheer-leader. That means I will be encouraging her. She has given me permission to interrupt her if I see something she might do or add that would be helpful to the lesson. Sometimes I might teach, or we might teach together, but my main role today is to cheer your teacher on.*

Give Students Specific Praise

Celebration also means giving useful and precise feedback. For example the following language is purposely specific: "*I noticed that Carl used really interesting words to describe how he plays with his dog. He didn't just say, 'I play with my dog.' He said, 'We wrestle. We lunge at each other.' I can really picture that.*" This kind of specific praise will have all the kids striving to use more interesting word choices in their writing. They will also be thinking, "If Carl can do that, so can I!"

Celebration of specific strengths—not idle praise—helps ensure early success for our students. Through whole-class sharing, small-group work, one-on-one conferences, and every other way we respond to students all day every day, we need to give them the message that they are capable.

Celebrate Small Accomplishments

Many of our students, especially the struggling ones, don't see their strengths and incremental improvements, so it's important to notice and point out what they have done well, even if it's a very small thing. These small celebrations can change the way learners view themselves and the way others view them. Often, those celebrations can even lead to increased engagement, confidence, and willingness to take risks. Time and time again, I have seen celebration jump-start greater learning and achievement. This is as true for us teachers as for students.

I will never forget a colleague telling me how devastated she was when her principal said to her, "I wish you could have done more with Jolene." My friend came to me in tears:

> *If only she had said, "Thank you for all your efforts with Jolene." I never worked harder with a student, but those words, "I wish you could have done more," caused me to retire a year early. I felt my efforts were unappreciated.*

Noticing what's done well can change a child's life. In a first-grade classroom, in a school where thirty languages were spoken, I called Tyana, who was sitting off to the side, under a desk, to come to the front of the class to share her written story. Students had been asked to extend our class text, "What We're Great At."

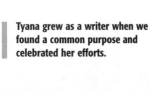

Tyana grew as a writer when we found a common purpose and celebrated her efforts.

As soon as Tyana began to move slowly toward the front of the classroom, I silently berated myself for selecting her. She was the largest student in the room, her eyes were downcast, and she projected a strong feeling of sadness. The last thing I wanted was to add to her discomfort.

Nevertheless, I asked her to read her story, which was about carving a pumpkin. After she read it and I asked a few questions, I realized she had probably never carved a pumpkin. Choosing my words carefully, I said to her, "I can tell you like pumpkins and you would like to carve one. What do you like about pumpkins?" From there, I helped her orally rehearse a few sentences about pumpkins, and she went back and wrote them down. Then I followed up with more celebration, giving Tyana specific comments about the work she had done: "Good for you. You took the sentences we were talking about and got them down on your paper."

Over the course of the weeklong residency, all of the teachers in the classroom noticed a huge change in Tyana's demeanor. She began to smile; she sat closer to the front of the room when the class gathered on the rug; she joined in as the students responded to shared experiences. She moved from making herself invisible to visible, and she did it on her own once she felt affirmed.

Make Celebration Part of Everything You Do

Celebration is about finding the joy in teaching and learning and "seeing" the child's accomplishments, no matter how small. When kids hear you compliment a student honestly, they will be thinking, "If she cares that much about so-and-so, she must also care that much about me," or, "She thinks what so-and-so did was terrific. I can do that too."

Celebration is not a frill. It's an essential part of all effective teaching. In my school residencies I always start the week by talking about the importance of celebration. At one school, first-grade teacher Mary Yuhas later told me what she and others were thinking:

> *When you first talked about celebration, we were all thinking, "We don't have time for that joy thing. We have the standards, required curriculum, and we're stretched to the limit." But by the end of the week, we saw that the joy thing was everything.*

Let the celebrations begin—and continue!

> *I will become the master of my craft as a teacher of reading and writing."*
>
> —JANE CURRY, GRADE 1–2 TEACHER

CHAPTER 3

Become an
"Expert at Smartness"

SEVERAL YEARS AGO I RECEIVED A LETTER from a third grader (see below). I was struck by her line, "You are an expert at smartness." I keep the letter posted by my desk as a source of encouragement on all those days I don't feel very smart and, also, as a reminder of how important it is to be smart about the professional work we do. By smartness I mean having the knowledge, leadership, common sense, people skills, and experience necessary to be an effective educator and communicator.

Like law and medicine (or any other profession in which it is essential to "keep up" in order to perform at the highest level of effi-cacy), teaching requires professional read-ing, collaboration with colleagues, coaching, sifting through the latest research, attending conferences, and so on. Without that level of smartness and engagement, we are at the mercy of the latest published program or "scientific" study and limited to following proce-dures without understanding them.

The same is true for our stu-dents, especially those who have no

> *Drop everything, whatever it takes—get into classrooms daily. You must observe, monitor, and partici-pate in the teaching/learning process. It's one of the best investments you can make in student achievement."*
>
> —BARBARA STALLINGS, PRINCIPAL IN A K–5 TITLE 1 SCHOOL

10-7-03
Dear Mrs. Routman,
You have a lot of skills inside of you. I don't know where you get all this info stuff. your one smart lady. your wonderfull. you are a expert at smanntess.

from your friend. Sean
For Mrs. Routman

role models for how to break out of the cycle of poverty, who struggle with learning English as a second language, and whose education has been stunted due to meager expectations. Smartness is everything.

Engage in **Professional** Study

When I first began my weeklong teaching and coaching residencies, I noticed that the energy at the end of the week was always high. Teachers and principals felt empowered. They had an "I can do it!" spirit as well as strategies and ideas for raising expectations, improving instruction and assessment, and making teaching more manageable and enjoyable. I would leave the school feeling confident that big changes were underway. However, when I returned to a school six months or a year later for a follow-up residency, nothing much had changed. The residency, in effect, was another "one-shot deal," just a longer one. New activities might be in place, but there was little understanding of how those activities fit within an Optimal Learning Model (see inside front cover and abridged version below). For example, teachers might have added shared writing to their repertoire as an activity, but not as a necessary scaffold to support learners so they could become more capable, confident, and independent.

I decided at that point not to return to a school unless the staff made a commitment to weekly professional conversations. The residency at its best is a catalyst for change. The real work of knowledge building happens on-site, day by day and week by week, thoughtfully, over time. Lasting student achievement occurs in schools where the principal and the teachers collaborate to make ongoing professional study a reality. Only when we combine the *what* and *how* of what we do with the *why* do we see permanent gains.

If we're not professionally smart, we may not know what new research means for our teaching or what we're "seeing" when we look at student work. I've been in schools where teachers get together and spend hours

THE OPTIMAL LEARNING MODEL

Teaching and Learning Contexts	Who Holds Book/Pen	Degree of Explicitness/Support
Celebration & Assessment Are Embedded		
Reading and Writing Aloud	**Teacher**/Student	**Demonstration**
Shared Reading and Writing Scaffolded Conversations	**Teacher**/Student	**Shared Demonstration**
gradual handover of responsibility		
Guided Reading Literature Conversations Reading/Writing Conferences	**Student**/Teacher	**Guided Practice**
Independent Reading/Writing	**Student**/Teacher	**Independent Practice**
Celebration & Assessment Are Embedded		

looking at students' writing, but their expectations are too low or there is an overfocus on skills, so what they "see," value, assess, and teach winds up not helping students move forward. *Professional development must help students learn more.* It is not enough that teachers become more confident and more knowledgeable about content. We must see results in increased student achievement throughout a whole school and district.

Likewise, in teaching reading, it's not enough to "have" guided reading groups, practice comprehension strategies, and provide time for voluntary reading. We have to document that students are becoming better readers, not just passing through levels. I will never forget sitting down with a third grader who had gotten 100 percent on a computerized reading test but who was unable to tell me the problem in the story, describe the setting, recount how the story ended, or explain key vocabulary. It was also an eye-opening experience for the observing teachers, who assumed the student was "progressing" because he could answer literal questions.

> *"It is not enough that teachers become more confident and more knowledgeable about content. We must see results in increased student achievement throughout a whole school and district."*

Get Professional Conversations Going

In a decade of working in schools across the country, I have learned that high achievement schoolwide only happens when there are collaboration and conversation throughout the whole school, across all grade levels and disciplines. A star teacher here and there whose students are high achievers does not impact lasting, schoolwide achievement.

Even if there is only one other colleague at your school who is interested, start meeting and talking about issues of the profession, the latest research, and effective teaching practices. Be invitational. Post an agenda. Share professional articles. I cannot stress enough how critical such conversations are for examining schoolwide issues and data, sharing what's going well, setting goals for improving instruction, and building the necessary collegiality for high achievement.

More than almost any other factor, the sense of a professional school community enhances student achievement. Studies have demonstrated that schools and districts that promote strong professional learning communities enable teachers to respond more successfully to the needs of students and to sustain positive change. These studies also confirm that schools and districts with weak professional learning communities are instructionally ineffective. (Moffett, 2000; see my website for recommended resources and titles to support being and becoming professionally knowledgeable.)

A page from my reading record.

Remain a Learner

What are the last books you have read? Are you making time to read professionally and personally? One of the first questions I would ask any teacher seeking employment is, *What are you reading? What is your last favorite book? How do you choose books? What have you learned as a reader?* Or, *Talk about a book or text that had a lasting impact on you, and tell why.*

I began keeping a reading record in 1993, and I treasure my reading history (a recent page is shown left). Each month I note the books, authors, and genres I have read and put an asterisk next to those I deem outstanding. Keeping a reading record has helped me balance what I read, and I help students implement a reading record with a similar format and similar goals.

I no longer read primarily professional books and educational journals. I also read memoir, nonfiction, history, poetry, essays, short stories, newspapers, and literary magazines. I need that balance to become knowledgeable in areas besides education and to be a more interesting person.

All teachers benefit from refocusing and self-evaluating.

View Teaching as a Craft

There's lots of pressure these days to view teaching mainly as a science that relies on "evidence-based" research and as an accumulation of predetermined skills to be taught in a hierarchy. When a scientific view dominates federal policies, it's up to us as educators to provide the needed balance. For example, while phonemic awareness, phonics, fluency, vocabulary, and comprehension are required elements in teaching early reading, wise teachers know that students also need to have lots of time to read self-selected literature at their "just right" level, have many opportunities to interact with peers (as well as the teacher) in small groups to talk deeply about texts, receive adequate background knowledge before listening to or reading a text, observe how an expert reader thinks her/his way through a text, and much more.

Just as competent practitioners in the professions of law, medicine, and architecture are known for their continuous study, mentoring, and wise application of wide experiences, the same must be true for us in the profession of teaching. The evaluation form shown left contains the thoughtful comments of a teacher who, at the end of a residency, realizes she needs to refocus her efforts as a teacher.

Align Your **Beliefs** with Your **Practices**

"My experience has been that until all the teachers in a school and/or district recognize where their beliefs diverge—and then align behind commonly held beliefs, high achievement remains out of reach."

Consider devoting an upcoming staff meeting to sharing beliefs on literacy learning. Our beliefs drive our teaching practices whether or not we articulate them, so bringing those beliefs out in the open can have profound effects on our teaching. Discuss, chart, and notice areas of agreement—and disagreement. Look at what you've written on the chart paper as a group. What do you see? Where might this lead you in terms of next conversations, next steps? This initial conversation is a crucial first step in making needed change. My experience has been that until all the teachers in a school and/or district recognize where their beliefs diverge—and then align behind commonly held beliefs, high achievement remains out of reach. Why? Because common beliefs create a coherent vision that in turn drives coherent teaching practices across the grades. Without that synchronicity, it's like hearing an orchestra warming up as opposed to *playing* a Stravinsky symphony.

There is a theory of insanity postulated by Albert Einstein: if you keep on doing what's not working, you're going to keep on getting the same results. If the test scores are low or remain flat, if the students hate and fear writing, if students are not applying the reading strategies we're teaching, we need to change course. Sadly, many of us continue on the same path even when things are going badly because we don't know what else to do or because learned helplessness, often accompanied by fear, has set in.

Examine Your Beliefs and Keep an Open Mind

At one school where most of the students are nonwhite and come from families with low incomes, achievement, as measured by tests and work samples, is dismal. Yet teachers continue drilling students on skills in isolation as they have always done. Even when these teachers see dramatic improvement in students' writing during my residency that focuses on whole-part-whole learning, they hold fast to those teaching-in-isolation beliefs.

I used to think that when teachers saw the dramatic achievements their students were capable of during a residency, they would change their practices. Not so. As I said before, but it bears restating, we all teach from a firmly held beliefs system whether we articulate those beliefs or not. As an example, many teachers in the intermediate grades believe that students are best served in ability groups, despite the fact that research does not support such grouping once students are readers. So it's a necessity that individually, schoolwide, and districtwide, those beliefs be continually examined, articulated, and discussed. Our beliefs determine our teaching practices.

Keep on open mind. Be willing to change your views when research and experience warrant it. I find that most teachers and administrators are open to new possibilities. The few exceptions are those who hold on to rigid and inflexible behavior and are unable, for whatever reasons, to alter and adjust their beliefs and practices—even when presented with evidence that does not support their current methods. We teachers must also believe that we are still learners, capable of acting on new knowledge.

Rely on **Common Sense**

Very often, at the end of a residency, teachers comment, "But what you do is common sense." And I respond, "Since when is common sense not allowed in teaching?" So many requirements cause us to teach in a frenzy and rely on others' judgments. If something seems like a ridiculous practice and waste of time, it probably is. Unfortunately, because most of us have so much on our plates—and, rarely, is anything ever taken away—we end up going along with practices, materials, and procedures that are not good for children, mostly because we are exhausted. Nonetheless, as educators, we need to be the gatekeepers for sane and sensible practices. Keep in mind, too, that even sound new research that enters our field should not completely engulf our practices; rather it should inform it. Research should help us raise fresh questions about teaching and learning that help us make smart instructional decisions to improve our practices. Too often, tried and true practices get entirely and unnecessarily pushed out of the classroom. Again, we are professionals and need to believe in our knowledge of what works in our classrooms, for our particular students.

Notice and Value What You Do as a Reader and Writer

While it's true that in teaching reading we need to focus on phonics, fluency, and comprehension (among other things), we also need to focus on ourselves as readers and writers and think about the strategies we use and why we use them. As readers of nonfiction, for example, we skim, scan,

"Teachers are the only professionals I know who will do what we know is not beneficial for our clients— our students and their families—rather than challenge obviously ineffective current ideas or new programs."

reread, look at headings and charts, figure out vocabulary, connect to personal experiences, set our ideas up against those of the authors, think and question as we read, and a whole lot more. It stands to reason that our teaching practices might mirror those reading tendencies. We need to weed out strategies that don't make sense.

When we read fiction, we set out to get lost in a book. We often unconsciously make connections between the character's lives and our own, and use our background knowledge to make sense of and engage with the story world. As a reader, I for one am not methodically predicting what is going to happen next or slowing down in any way to link what I'm reading to another book. With a great book, the author's words carry me along and I am in a flow of total engagement and enjoyment. And so when I go to teach reading to understand narrative, you won't find me overdoing pause-and-predict work or stopping to teach strategies in isolation. Be true to your own reading habits.

Similarly, as writers, we often jot down ideas, draft, revise, and edit as we go along, write with our reader(s) in mind, and rarely use a graphic organizer to plan before we write. We need to show and explain to our students the strategies we use to understand and compose text and to note that we use these interactively, not one at a time. In other words, when teaching strategies, as is true of teaching anything, keep it real, and use what you do as reader and a writer to restore balance to your teaching practices. One key question to keep in mind for all our teaching: Is this a practice that occurs in the real world? If it's just a school thing, we need to question the practice.

We also need to apply common sense and give credence to and spend time on practices we know work: the importance of the reading/writing connection for helping kids become better readers and writers and doing so more quickly, the power of social networks such as partner reading for improving reading, the necessity for free-choice voluntary reading and writing supported by wonderful classroom libraries, and the revision and editing efforts students willingly make when they write for authentic and valued audiences and purposes. And that's just for starters.

Advocate for Your Students

Teachers are the only professionals I know who will do what we know is not beneficial for our clients—our students and their families—rather than challenge obviously ineffective current ideas or new programs. We must as responsible educators be advocates for our students. Remember, the district that may be mandating questionable and in some cases harmful practices is *your* district, and someone in your district office—often with input from teachers and principals—determined that mandate. Rather than jumping through hoops demonstrating your fidelity to the latest program, put your energy into expressing your fidelity to your students.

Some examples include using Dibels and timed fluency exercises (without comprehension) and teaching with texts that we know are too difficult for most of the kids. Even though there is overwhelming research showing that Dibels does not improve reading achievement (see my website for the particulars), educators in many states continue to use the assessment, spending countless dollars and hours that could go to far better use.

Renowned educational researcher Richard Allington advocates that we examine our state's code of ethics for teachers (available on your state department of education's website) and use that code to disavow unprofessional practices. He goes so far as to recommend that we say, "Please put in writing that you want me to violate the state code of professional ethics."

It takes courage to take a stand for what we believe is best for kids, and it takes energy, but it takes more energy to continue going along with senseless, time-consuming practices. Playwright Arthur Miller astutely noted:

> *The longer I worked the more certain I felt that as improbable as it might seem, there were moments when an individual conscience was all that could keep a world from falling. (Herbert, The New York Times, 2005)*

Conserve Time and Energy

Be protective of the limited time you have. Avoid elaborate centers, overlong assignments, cute activities that take lots of time but teach little of importance, complex directions that need to be restated, and so on. Keep asking yourself, *How is what I am expecting students to do helping them become more proficient, confident, and independent as learners?* And: *What are students learning? How do I know?*

I advise principals to keep the same questions in mind. The only way to get into classrooms each day and know what supports are needed for teachers and students is to put children and teachers first and paperwork second. Completing paperwork and remaining glued to the computer most of the day will not raise student achievement. One principal I greatly admire told me how she gets out of her office and into classrooms every day. How does she find the time? "I wait until a request from central office is repeated. If there's a third request, I know it must be important, and then I respond."

Eliminate distractions that are within your control. Advocate for a school policy that minimizes interruptions and announcements except

for crucial events. Work to keep all your students with you, in the classroom, during rich language activities such as read-aloud, shared reading, and shared writing. Make classroom procedures clear and easy to follow. For example, do not allow kids to get up and sharpen pencils during writing time—it's a distraction and time waster. Have a can of sharpened pencils ready to go.

Budget your time. Use a timer; be mindful of the clock. You can't teach everything in one lesson. Stop when kids' energy is still high. Teachers are often surprised when I stop a demonstration or shared writing after ten minutes and finish up the next day. Teachers tell me, "I would have run that lesson into the ground and stopped when I and the kids were exhausted." Remember that students need to spend most of their time and energy on daily sustained practice if they are going to learn and apply what we are teaching them.

Place more responsibility on the kids, which saves time and energy and makes them more independent. Use the Optimal Learning Model to teach students how to partner-read, self-edit, fix-up misspelled words, peer conference, self-direct small groups, follow procedures, find resources, and so on.

Communicate with Stakeholders

Promote and value positive public relations. Share how you teach, what you are teaching, and why you are teaching it before you begin a new unit or focus. Use a shared writing or monthly newsletter or individual letters written by students to communicate what students are studying and learning. (An example is AlexSandra's newsletter on p. 22). Her parents can clearly see she is now a competent writer and speller.

Families are often confused because we have not been clear enough about what's going on. The bulletin boards in your room and in the school, the work you send home, the homework you assign, all send a message about what you value, what you expect, and what you are teaching. For example, if your walls are covered with commercially produced resources but little class-generated work, it sends a message that you value visual reference material but that you don't give celebrating students' work a high priority. If the homework assigned is mostly skills worksheets, parents get the message that skill and drill lead to learning. Ensure that the work you display, assign, and share with families affirms and celebrates children's strengths, interests, histories, and culture in the home, the classroom, and school.

Communicate with parents before problems arise. Make phone calls early in the school year with a compliment about each student, explain the use of invented spelling by young writers before papers go home, share required rubrics and grading guidelines, and so on. Establish a relationship with parents prior to school-mandated conferences so they are comfortable talking with you about their child. If concerns later arise, the parent will be more likely to listen without becoming defensive.

Publish often. Use shared writing weekly to create shared reading texts that become independent reading texts. Make publishing a regular classroom activity. Work with students to publish lots of short pieces with real-world audiences—book reviews, op-ed pieces, advice to new students, about the author (the student), classroom procedures, letters of appreciation—that give students the repeated practice they need revising and editing and that let parents see what we are teaching and what kids are learning.

Take a **Leadership** Role

Learned helplessness is part of the culture of many schools. Over and over, teachers tell me what they "have to"do. Often, with probing, I learn that they could adjust a policy, do the assessment in a slightly different way, and create some flexibility if they took a leadership role. By being proactive and suggesting alternative ways an administrator can get the required information, we can break out of the role of victim. Also, when we see firsthand that a district policy or program is not helping increase student achievement, we need to question that policy and at the same time offer to collaboratively seek out workable alternatives.

Use Programs as a Resource

As responsible educators and advocates for our students, it is our job to question the research and ask the hard questions before any new program or textbook is adopted. (My website contains some useful questions and guidelines.) For example, we need to be aware that many people who generate textbooks and supplemental programs have little or no teaching experience; slick sales and marketing campaigns often cause programs and resources to be approved in districts without first testing in schools; programs marketed for all students may have been developed primarily for special education students or based on one particular state's curriculum mandates.

Even when a program has passed muster, we must provide a balance by using a variety of excellent resources. If we have very limited resources, we can use the public library to help shore up our classroom library with books and resources on topics that kids are interested in and that support our curriculum. When any one textbook becomes the total curriculum, we shortchange students.

Most programs, at best, provide a framework and basic knowledge; even then, caution and judgment in program use and implementation are essential. Knowledgeable teachers and administrators carefully pick the best parts of any adopted program and ignore the unfavorable features. This is also how you can make it your own, and ensure you are considering the unique interests of the students in your classroom.

Recognize Colleagues' Strengths

The first thing I do in a new residency is make the rounds; the principal and I go into every classroom and I meet each teacher. Although I will only be demonstrating and coaching in two classrooms (one primary and one intermediate), I want every one of the observing teachers to know I

Observation is the first step in my residencies, done in a trusting, collegial environment.

value them. When I walk into their classrooms, I am on the lookout for something positive—a wonderful classroom library, a beautiful room arrangement, kids that seem engaged, a cozy reading area, an accessible word wall—and I briefly and honestly comment on it.

It's all about relationships. I've learned that if we don't have positive, trusting relationships with our colleagues and students, not much of any consequence is likely to happen. On the other hand, when we do have that trust, we can ask for and expect more from our colleagues and students. That mutual trust implies the support will be there when it is needed. Principals and teachers need to continue to work together to establish expectations for creating and sustaining a safe, supportive, collegial environment.

If you are a teacher or principal who is new to a school, look at your colleagues through a wide lens of acceptance. Focus on what's going well before addressing concerns. And, first, actively listen. A kindergarten teacher once asked me early in the school year, "So what do you think of my word wall?" Actually, the number of words on it (sixty) as well as the frenetic look of the thing (each word was artfully illustrated and it took up the length and height of one side of her classroom) stunned me. I held my tongue and asked instead, "What would you like to know about it?" She described how excited she was about her word wall and how well it was working. Now I understood. She wanted affirmation, not honest feedback. "Well," I truthfully told her, "It looks beautiful. You've sure done a lot of work here. I'm glad it's working for you." She beamed. I left it at that.

The following school year, the same kindergarten teacher sought me out and asked, "What do you really think of my word wall?" Again, I asked her what she wanted to know. This time she said, "I think I may have too many words here for kindergartners. I'm wondering if that might be distracting for some of them." Now that we had a trusting relationship, she was ready and willing to take an honest look at her word wall. It was no longer just about the word wall; it was about what was instructionally best for her students.

Get to know all your colleagues. Observe respected colleagues at other grade levels. Adopt a coaching-partnering model (see Chapter 7). Mentor colleagues and seek out a mentor yourself. I have always believed that mentoring is part of our job as teachers, whether we are paid or not, and that we have an unspoken obligation to support our peers. Even if you are not assigned a mentor, and especially if you are new to teaching, try to find a teacher in your building that you admire and can learn from.

"I've learned that if we don't have positive, trusting relationships with our colleagues and students, not much of any consequence is likely to happen."

Acknowledge the Significant Role of the Principal

My admiration for principals is enormous. I know firsthand that most work twelve-hour days; do whatever they can to support their teachers, their students, and their students' families; and sometimes have little support from the central office. Principals, like teachers, are my heroes.

In a decade of working with schools and districts, perhaps the most important thing I've learned about school achievement is that the principal is the pivotal factor. Principal leadership and knowledge are a requirement. This is a tough reality to accept. I used to think that strong teacher leadership in a building was sufficient to move a school forward, but my experience does not support that belief. Without exception, I have found that only with strong principal leadership do schools move toward and maintain high achievement.

Teachers must do all they can to support and encourage their principals, especially unseasoned ones, to be strong, collegial leaders. For example, bring your principal terrific professional articles to help him/her stay abreast of current research and best practices. Before a classroom observation, tell your principal the purpose of your lesson and how you will be teaching and assessing all students so the principal knows what to look for and is focused on big understandings. Have your students explain why they're doing what they're doing. Seeing firsthand what a student is able to do can change a principal's perspective. Take every opportunity you can to forge a strong, trusting relationship with the principal.

Administrators, like teachers, must take responsibility for learning what excellent literacy practices look like and sound like, focusing on continuous whole-staff (both at and across grade levels) in-house professional development, and supporting all teachers in applying effective literacy practices.

Use Technology Wisely

Finally, a word about technology. Technology is great as long as it's attached to authentic teaching and learning. To be beneficial, technology has to make our teaching lives easier and more productive as well as increase student learning. So many schools have heavily invested in the latest technology and glitzy programs without improving academic achievement. Remember the computerized reading program I mentioned earlier that offered no comprehension?

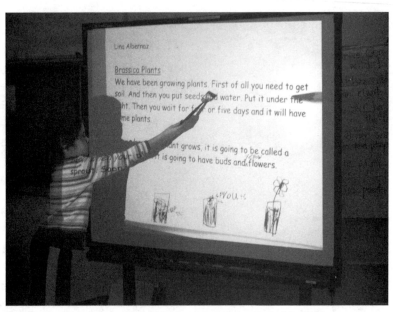

Lina Albernaz

Brassica Plants
We have been growing plants. First of all you need to get
soil. And then you put seeds and water. Put it under the
ht. Then you wait for f or five days and it will have
me plants.

nt grows, it is going to be called a
t is going to have buds and flowers.

| Technology at its best involves students and teachers in meaningful activities.

In a recent residency, the school in which I was working was techno-
logically wired in every way (laptops for every teacher, electronic white
boards in every classroom that made it possible to display any text, curriculum and lesson plans on a district website). Nevertheless, I was struck
by how little the teachers knew about effective teaching. They were sophisticated users of technology, but that did not translate to better teaching.
Technology can be a magnificent tool but to be an effective one, we teachers have to know the latest research, how to teach and assess, how to meet
the needs of all our students, and so on.

Some effective uses of technology include videotaping your teaching, online collaboration, creating websites for your school and district
that showcase student work, communicating staff information in emails
and saving staff meetings for professional development, enlarging selected
pages of text for shared read-aloud, publishing student work, teaching
students to use digital photos and/or PowerPoint or iMovie for presentations, posting lessons or assessments for other teachers to use, posting
curricular documents online, and creating electronic bulletin boards
where staff can give feedback to curriculum developers.

First, however, put your money and efforts into developing magnificent school and classroom libraries. Access to books and a wide variety
of excellent reading materials and genres have the potential to do more to
increase achievement than any advanced technology. Reading and writing

excellent literature can and do increase student learning; the research is far less clear for technology. And we must remember that the ease and proliferation of search engines for fact-finding and possibly plagiarism are real issues in our classrooms. We need to teach students how to use technology wisely, not just copy and paste. Not only that, there is something we gain from holding and reading a book in our hands that has the power to transcend technology and even surpass it—we need to model this experience for our students:

> *It is interesting to me in an age of blogs, Webs, and texting that a book, something that is essentially a tortoise, very quaint in its own way, can carry the most immediacy. (Rosenthal,* The New York Times, *2006)*

As in all areas of teaching where you want to be influential, be knowledgeable about technology; take a leadership role regarding it; communicate your views and opinions about it clearly; and apply common sense, smart thinking, and experience in its use.

The change in that child, in her level of confidence and in her academic progress is remarkable and inspiring."

—NANCY McLEAN, LITERACY COACH

CHAPTER 4

Focus on
Meaning First

MIDYEAR IN A KINDERGARTEN CLASSROOM, many children were pronouncing words without attaching meaning to them. Just about all the children could read a few words in their reading books, but being able to talk about what they had just read was another matter. Carlos, a developing reader, proudly read every word correctly in his leveled text. "What's it about?" I asked. No response. "What's happening in the story?" He looked up at me but made no reply. "Let's take a look at the cover and the pictures together. What do you think is happening?" It was a simple story about baking a fancy birthday cake for a queen. We talked the story through together, connecting the words with the pictures. "Carlos," I told him. "Whenever you're reading, it has to make sense."

Babies come into the world trying to make sense of it. Young children can read and listen for meaning even if they don't know all their letters and sounds and understand every word. As human beings, we always seek to make meaning; it's literally how we are wired. Neuroscience research in the last decades has revealed more and more about the human brain's pattern-seeking. If we focus on meaning and content first with our students, we can't help but succeed and teach all the necessary skills.

> *I grew up as bilingual-bicultural and have been teaching for two decades. It grieves me to see that for many of our English language learners, instruction continues to be meaningless, out of context, and outside the mainstream classroom—just as it was for me."*
>
> —SANDRA GARCIA,
> TEACHER OF ENGLISH
> LANGUAGE LEARNERS
> AND LITERACY COACH

Whether working with kindergartners or adolescents, I start with a meaningful whole. I talk about the text we are going to read or write, whether it's a poem, a shared writing, a letter, or a book. It never ceases to amaze me how much and how quickly children can learn when the purpose is clear and relevant, the content makes sense, and we provide enough demonstrations, support, and time for guided and independent practice.

Rely on a **Whole-Part-Whole** Teaching Approach

A teacher recently wrote me that she had no "flow" in her classroom. She was doing shared reading and shared writing and teaching skills and strategies, but her teaching seemed broken into bits and pieces. Try as she might, she was unable to make her teaching seamless: "I don't know how to connect the dots."

When I go into classrooms, it is common to find all the components of a reading or writing program in place in a "literacy block"—phonics and word study, guided reading, independent reading, revision, editing, writing traits, and so on. Implementation involves lots of separate pieces, but often the parts are not connected and integrated into a meaningful whole. Students don't "see" how the parts are connected, and they fail to apply what they are being taught to their daily work. Not surprisingly, student achievement remains flat. As one teacher told me, "I teach them all about capitals and periods, but they don't use them much when they write." Sometimes the problem is from the top down: the school and district lack a comprehensive curricular plan that makes sense to teachers and students. But we can change that in our own classrooms.

In my weeklong residencies, the biggest shift teachers make in their effort to transform their teaching is to move from teaching in small pieces to a whole-part-whole teaching philosophy and approach. That is, instead of focusing on skills in isolation, they focus first on a meaningful whole. All the skills are explicitly taught, but in a way that is connected and necessary to doing and understanding the whole text or task. Think about it. If we don't place the pieces and routines of literacy into a natural, meaningful context, it's like a story devoid of setting, a Renoir painting without a background—there is not enough to compel a young learner, not enough to stir his or her curiosity.

We always need to be thinking and asking ourselves, *Is what I'm doing compelling? How is what I'm doing helping kids become more effective, independent, and joyful as readers, writers, thinkers, problem solvers?* Instead we are often asking, *What skills do I need to teach to meet the standards? How can I get my students to write a paragraph? How can we raise test scores?*

The whole really is greater than the sum of its parts. You can teach more in less time when you start with a meaningful whole. Also, teachers and students are more likely to be efficient and engaged as well as experience more enjoyment. You do have to know what skills, concepts, and strategies your particular students need to learn in order to be successful, but these need not be taught in isolation, one by one.

Start with Relevant Purpose

"The whole really is greater than the sum of its parts. You can teach more in less time when you start with a meaningful whole."

We all invest our energies more when we understand and value the purpose of what we are doing. A personal story illustrates the point. Several years ago, my husband Frank and I were about to move from Cleveland to Seattle to be closer to our son Peter, his wife Claudine, and our grandchildren. We were sprucing up our condominium so it would sell quickly. Each day Frank would ask me to wipe up the water that had dripped from the hand-washed dishes in the plastic drainer onto the tile kitchen counter. I ignored him, thinking, "If he wants to, fine. I'm not taking the time to do that." But one day he said to me,

> The reason I've asked you to dry the counter is because the grout in between the tiles is coming loose, especially where the counter and tile wall come together. Some of the tiles might break off. If we don't keep the counter dry, we may need to replace the tiles, and that would be expensive.

Ah, now I understood—and complied. Problem solved. So it is with our students. If we want their best efforts, they need to understand why they're undertaking a task or reading a text: it has to make sense to them.

When I begin a new residency, I always ask the children, "Do you know why I'm here?" Often they don't. Or, when we have whole-class public conferences after writing, I explain the purpose of the conferences—first, celebration and, then, to make possible suggestions to help the writer. Always, before we begin a lesson or activity, I make sure students are clear about the purpose. *Why are we having conferences today? What's the reason we're reading this together? Why is it important that your editing be as perfect as you can get it? Why is it important to reread?*

Use Authentic Reading and Writing Activities

Most of my planning consists of trying to figure out how to make reading and writing as authentic and purposeful for students as possible. Once I have that authenticity, I can teach anything.

Nell Duke and other researchers (Duke et al., 2006/2007) define authentic, classroom literacy activities as

> . . . those that replicate or reflect reading and writing activities that occur in the lives of people outside of a learning-to-read-and-write context and purpose. Each authentic literacy activity has a writer and a reader—a writer who is writing to real reader and a reader who is reading what the writer wrote. (p. 346)

These researchers also report that adults enrolled in literacy programs with authentic reading and writing activities report reading and writing more in their lives and reading and writing more complex texts (p. 345). My experience as a teacher-researcher has been that students of all ages read and write more and with greater quality and independence when the task and the text are authentic and relevant.

I always have students write for a real audience and purpose, and that alone has done more to improve writing quality than any other factor. Students are willing to do the hard work of revising and editing because they know and care about their reader. Their investment in the task propels them to put forth their best efforts.

For example, when writing book reviews (not book reports, which only exist in schools), our main purpose may be to begin to teach summarizing. Even though that purpose may be mostly related to meeting standards and district requirements, establishing a meaningful student purpose and audience is central to full student engagement and effort. We examine book reviews as they appear in the world, talk about how and why they are written, determine criteria (a rubric) for writing one, write one together, and then the students write one of their own on a recent favorite book. Students plan ahead of time and specifically determine the purpose and audience for the reviews they are about to write. We have written book reviews at all grade levels and compiled them so that other kids in the classroom can refer to them when selecting a book to read, shared them with other classes, posted them on Amazon.com, displayed them at local book stores, and added them to a school/district website devoted to recommended reading.

And, again, in reading I ensure that most of our daily reading time is spent actually reading self-selected fiction and nonfiction and not primarily in reading groups, writing answers to lots of questions, or doing activities about reading. In reading literature, we need to hold tight to oral and written discourse that is real world, not school world. For example, when I pose questions about a book or share what I wonder, my comments sound just like the ones I'd make to a friend who had just read the same book. I ask, and I teach students to ask and respond to, "big," important questions as they read, when they meet in self-directed, small group literature conversations, or when they express their thinking in a response journal. A few examples of provocative questions that cause students to read closely and to reread might include:

- What motivated the character to behave the way s/he did?

- What is the author trying to tell the reader about _____?

- I wonder if the author believes people are (born good and kind) or whether they learn to be (good and moral)?

- What are the most important things you learned about _____? How does that change your original thinking?

Interacting meaningfully with texts is essential if our students are to become not just literate beings who choose to read and write for worthwhile purposes but, also, thoughtful citizens who are able to connect and justify ideas, make meaningful interpretations, analyze multiple perspectives, explain their thinking, ask important questions, make new meanings, and take actions by applying their thinking to new situations.

Embed Skills as a Means to a Worthwhile End

We need to be able to teach more in less time. The only way we can teach efficiently and have enough time to teach what's necessary—curriculum, standards, all the discrete objectives—so all students achieve at high levels, is to teach multiple skills simultaneously and interactively, focusing on the parts as needed.

Every time I teach in a school, I find the hardest concept for teachers and administrators to grasp is that when we start with a meaningful whole and focus on a high degree of comprehension, all the skills will be taught in order to achieve the

Below are the skills we taught in just a few days in a grade 1 classroom (see photo) where all the students were English language learners. Focusing on writing a whole meaningful text (and embedding skills) raised expectations and student writing quality.

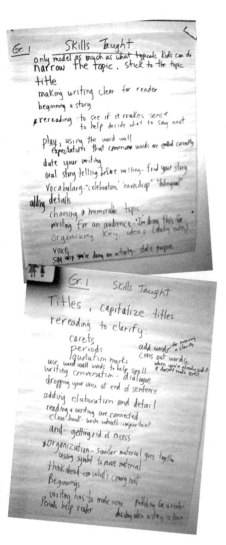

desired outcome. Conversely, when we start with isolated skills, it's easy to stay at the superficial level and for test scores and achievement to remain flat. Principals need to support teachers in moving beyond focusing on narrow objectives, including being sure they are using data analysis constructively. Too often data focus on missing pieces rather than on the big meaningful picture.

For example, instead of teaching topic sentences with supporting details, we can begin with a whole meaningful text for an audience and purpose that students value and understand. Students learn the necessary skills, not to do better on "the test," but because they need those skills to complete their meaningful work. When students and teachers mostly focus on the parts of a writing formula, the writing remains stilted, and improvement is minimal. Students do not automatically move beyond formulaic writing and reading. In other words, the skills aren't necessarily transferred to and applied in creating connected and extended texts. In fact, overemphasis on skills, such as phonics, can hamper a students' meaning making.

Provide More Demonstrations

THE OPTIMAL LEARNING MODEL

Teaching and Learning Contexts	Who Holds Book/Pen	Degree of Explicitness/Support
Celebration & Assessment Are Embedded		
Reading and Writing Aloud	**Teacher**/Student	**Demonstration**
Shared Reading and Writing Scaffolded Conversations	**Teacher**/Student	**Shared Demonstration**
gradual handover of responsibility		
Guided Reading Literature Conversations Reading/Writing Conferences	**Student**/Teacher	**Guided Practice**
Independent Reading/Writing	**Student**/Teacher	**Independent Practice**
Celebration & Assessment Are Embedded		

If we want students to tackle tasks and texts from the point of view of meaning and understanding, we have to show them explicitly what that looks like and sounds like, through a process of setting agreed upon learning purposes, thinking and doing out loud, providing time in which students can try out and practice these skills and providing opportunities for students to apply the demonstrations to actual reading and writing (what I commonly refer to as "Try It/Apply It").

AN EFFECTIVE DEMONSTRATION

- Explain *why* you are doing what you are about to undertake.
- Think aloud as you are modeling so students hear your in-the-head processes.
- Only demonstrate as much as the majority of students are capable of doing at this time.
- Check to see whether students "got" your demonstration. Have them say back to you what you did or what you expect them to do.
  - *What did you notice?*
  - *What did you see me do?*
  - *What do I expect you to try/apply?*
- Be prepared to repeat and expand your demonstrations. Remember, one demonstration is rarely enough.
- Include scaffolded conversations between you and one or two students before expecting students to write.
- Have students talk to one another before attempting the task.
- Be available to help as students attempt what you have demonstrated.

In a writing residency with teachers who needed more guidelines on what an effective writing demonstration comprises, we did a shared writing together to define it.

Plan with the **End in Mind**

What is it we want our students to be able to do? Surely it is more than to learn phonemic awareness and phonics, learn to write with correct conventions, and learn to read with fluency. I believe we want our students to be readers, writers, and thinkers across the curriculum; to have the skills necessary to problem-solve, self-monitor, self-reflect, and adjust; and to choose to go on learning—not just in school but throughout their lives. We want them to engage and enjoy learning, not just experience unrelated activities.

By planning with the end in mind, I *do* mean identifying what we want the learner to know and be able to do; I *do not mean* teaching one focus, standard, or skill. The current narrow focus on "mastering" standards or predetermined skills has shortchanged our students, exhausted teachers and administrators, and had scant effect on sustaining achievement and applying learning to new contexts. If we truly want *all* our students to be successful, we cannot teach part-to-whole in small, incremental pieces; the process is inefficient, bores our students, takes too much time, and is often meaningless to the learner.

When I plan with the end in mind, I start with the students I am teaching and spend most of my time thinking about things like this:

- What are the students' needs and interests?
- How can I start with their strengths and build on them?
- How can I capture their minds and hearts?
- What culturally relevant literature can I use to support my teaching?
- How can I embrace an authentic purpose and audience?
- How can I make the required curriculum and standards meaningful?
- What immersion or background knowledge do I first need to provide?
- Where do I want them to be at the end of our study? (This includes content knowledge, ability to apply and transfer new learning, level of independence, willingness to take responsibility for learning, attitudes, and confidence level.) It was planning with the end in mind that made a dramatic difference for the "Dreams" students. (See pp. 12–15.)

In another example, during a recent writing residency in a school in California where 100 percent of the students came from low-income families and most were English language learners, I chose to focus on writing poetry in a fifth-grade classroom, even though it was not a required genre. Test scores and achievement at this school had been dismal for years in spite of the enormous, heartfelt effort by the teachers and principal to teach "the skills" and required genres. Students had just completed a required genre study on persuasive writing that had gone on for two months. The teacher was the primary audience for the students' writing, and the focus had been on following a rubric, written in adult language, including all the parts of a persuasive piece. Yet when I asked students, "Why do people write? What do people write?" and charted their responses, even with suggestive prompting, writing to persuade never came up. The unit they had worked so hard to complete was a school thing for them and had no connection to the real world.

By having the students write free verse, we not only taught them many skills they could transfer to all of their writing but also captured their interest and their desire to write and go on writing. The students easily made the connections their teachers were struggling to make: what good writers do is the same in all genres, and writing is something people do every day in the world. (See the evaluations below that students made of their learning.)

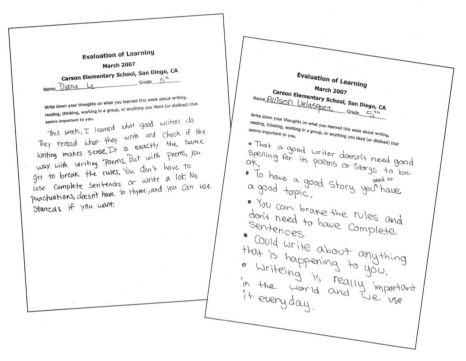

Evaluation of Learning
March 2007
Carson Elementary School, San Diego, CA
Name Diana Le   Grade 5th

Write down your thoughts on what you learned this week about writing, reading, thinking, working in a group, or anything you liked (or disliked) that seems important to you.

This week, I learned what good writers do. They reread what they write and check if the writing makes sense. It is exactly the same way with writing poems. But with poems, you get to break the rules. You don't have to use complete sentences or write a lot. No punctuations, doesn't have to rhyme, and you can use stanzas if you want.

Evaluation of Learning
March 2007
Carson Elementary School, San Diego, CA
Name Allison Velasquez   Grade 5th

Write down your thoughts on what you learned this week about writing, reading, thinking, working in a group, or anything you liked (or disliked) that seems important to you.

• That a good writer doesn't need good spelling for its poems or storys to be ok.
• To have a good story you need to have a good topic.
• You can brake the rules and don't need to have complete sentences.
• Could write about anything that is happening to you.
• Writeing is really important in the world and we use it everyday.

Start with the Student, Not the Standard

What matters most to this child? Start there. If the child is fascinated with snakes, bring in books and materials to support that interest. Focus the writing here for as long as necessary, even months. For example, the student can write a report on snakes, create a picture book describing different snakes, or prepare a guide on how to care for a snake. We can teach everything the student needs to know about reading and writing with a focus on what's most important to that child. That's why choice in writing is so important, why we need to negotiate the curriculum with our students, why study in the content areas must be relevant to kids' lives. Not only that, our teaching load is lightened because the students are more motivated, leading them to learn more quickly and making both their job and ours easier. I am always thinking, *What do I want students to know and be able to do?* but I am thinking globally and intentionally embedding the skills and standards in meaning. And I am thinking about the child.

Rebekah is a student I will always remember. I worked with her in a recent writing residency that took place in an urban school in a second-grade class of mostly English language learners. With many teachers and students observing, her teacher chose her to come to the front of the room to have a scaffolded conversation with me. I had just completed demonstrating my own storytelling and writing, about my cat Norman and our morning ritual of petting her on my lap while I drink my coffee. As I always do, through a back-and-forth public conversation, I wanted students to hear at least one elaborate story by a peer to spur their own thinking and ideas before they went off to write.

The whole class celebrates Rebekah right after she read her "Hide and Seek" story.

I knew nothing about Rebekah. Her head was downcast, and she was silent. No matter what I asked her in an effort to find out what she was interested in, there was no response. After ten minutes, I even wondered if she might be mute. It was one of the most difficult conferences I'd ever had. Still, I gently persisted, and finally thought to ask, "Do you have a mother?" She shook her head "yes," which was her first response to any question I'd posed. "Do you play with her?" Again, she nodded her head "yes." "What do you play?" No response. I kept on with more questions and finally asked (and got lucky,) "Do you play hide and seek with her?" She nodded. Now that we had a topic she was interested in, slowly, gently, and with much prodding, Rebekah began to tell her story in a barely audible whisper. This reticent child, who had experienced little academic success in school, wrote her story down without help, read it aloud in a public conference (to everyone's amazement), and began to blossom, gain confidence, and greatly improve as a reader and writer. Beginning with the whole student and what mattered in her life made it possible to teach her everything she needed to know to become literate.

When I saw Rebekah again several months later, she was all smiles, easily independently writing three to four pages in thirty minutes, enthusiastically talking about her work, and viewing herself as a capable student. The literacy coach commented, "Rebekah is a powerful example of what can happen when the teacher does not give up on a child and allows the child to read/write about her interests. The change in that child, in her level of confidence and in her academic progress, is remarkable and inspiring."

With all the pressures teachers are under, it can be really hard to take the time to patiently coax a child like Rebekah to reveal what matters to her. However, an extra minute or two with a child can make a world of difference, not just for the one child but for all the children who are listening in and observing.

Know and Apply the Standards

We teachers are experienced in delivering pretest instruction for high-stakes tests but far less experienced in making daily instruction riveting and relevant to our students. Of course, we do need to align the strategies we teach with state requirements and standards, but we can prioritize and reorder them. We can think of the standards more broadly, through a whole-part-whole lens, and put meaning first.

For example, in Washington state, where I live, the four main content standards for writing—called the Essential Academic Learning Requirements (EALRs)—are:

1. The student understands and uses the steps of the writing process.

2. The student writes in a variety of forms for different audiences and purposes.

3. The student writes clearly and effectively using traits of quality writing.

4. The student analyzes and evaluates the effectiveness of written work.

I move number 2 up to number 1 and list the others below it. Having "the student writes in a variety of forms for different audiences and purposes" as my primary concern changes everything: I can give writing instruction the meaningful focus students need and still teach all the required skills and standards.

In reading, our state content standards are:

1. The student understands and uses different skills and strategies to read.

2. The student understands the meaning of what is read.

3. The student reads different materials for a variety of purposes.

4. The student sets goals and evaluates progress to improve reading.

Again, I move number 2 to the top of the list: "The student understands the meaning of what is read."

Take a close look at your state standards. Don't let the way they are listed determine what's most important. Even when the state's focus is on skills first, start with meaning. You'll still be teaching all the required standards, and you'll be able to teach far more in less time and with greater enjoyment.

Teach It First; Label It Later

Basically, what we want for our students is the same, kindergarten through grade 12. As readers, we want them to choose books they can and want to read, read for various purposes, use reading to enrich their lives, read in various genres, be able to summarize and analyze what they read, and so on. As writers, we want them to write for meaningful purposes and valued audiences and to do that writing with voice, organization, fluency, correct conventions, interesting words, and so on. What changes from grade to grade are the length and complexity of the texts, the number of demonstrations and the amount of guided support students require, and the students' level of independence.

"When we attach labels before students have had enough immersion and practice, they rarely transfer what we are trying to teach them, because they don't understand how and why the strategy or concept is meaningful."

Always I find that when I teach what students need through demonstrations and shared and guided practice—but without labeling it with words and phrases such as "making connections," "adding transitions," and "summarizing"—students are far more likely to grasp these concepts and apply them to new contexts. When we attach labels before students have had enough immersion and practice, they rarely transfer what we are trying to teach them, because they don't understand how and why the strategy or concept is meaningful.

You only have so much time. When doing a demonstration, thinking out loud, or conducting a one-on-one or public conference, think, *What's most important to teach now? What do they know and need to know?* Keep your focus on the content and on demonstrating the thinking and reading/writing processes. When demonstrating writing, instead of saying, "I'm putting an exclamation mark here and adding details here," just do it. Or, when conferring with students, focus first on the student and the message he is trying to convey. Some teachers feel the need to teach everything at once—to focus on capitals and periods along with the message, for example. You can't teach everything in a ten- or fifteen-minute demonstration or conference, and if you try, you lose your focus, confuse the kids, and lose their attention. Also, the only way to move quickly and efficiently—so students have sufficient and sustained time to practice and apply what you are showing them—is to stay focused on what's most important.

When demonstrating summarizing, I read the text aloud to students and stop after every page or few pages and talk about the most important thing that's happening and how I made that decision. I explain that readers and writers need to know how to decide what's most important so a text makes sense and they also need to stop reading and reread or seek help when they don't know. Then, in keeping with the Optimal Learning Model, I use shared and guided opportunities to teach students to pick out the most important parts of a text. Once students can do this well, which typically takes several weeks or even months, I say, "What we've been learning and doing—deciding what the most important parts of the text are—is called summarizing." Now students have the background experience to understand what the term means.

In a similar vein, I do teach quotation marks, transitions, and so on starting in kindergarten, but I use these "parts" in service to making meaning and "just do it" as I focus on writing interesting content. Later on, once students have internalized these parts and how they are used, I say, even in kindergarten,

> *What we've been doing, adding a sentence in to let the reader know what's coming next, that's called a transition. Good writers use transitions to make their writing easier to follow and understand.*

What convinces teachers to teach it first, label it later, is noticing how many more skills we do teach and how efficient we are when we focus on meaning first. As an example, in a first-grade classroom where I was demonstrating how to write with elaboration and detail (but not naming it till later), observing teachers brainstormed what we had taught in just three days. The list shown on page 53 in the left margin is just how they generated it. Notice that the named skills apply to all grade levels. Had I set out to teach everything on the list, I would have exhausted myself. Planning with the end in mind and keeping the focus on a meaningful whole made it possible to teach the necessary skills in context.

Plan for Independence

No matter what the learning activity, try to set it up so that students are able to work as independently as possible. For example, guided reading, often viewed as the mainstay of a reading program, is one instructional context that can easily get offtrack. Students and teachers dutifully spend time in structured reading groups, but the teacher is often doing most of the work, and students not in groups are doing "busywork." However, if we plan with the end in mind, we set out with the goal that students will be able to read independently with understanding. Most of their time, therefore, must be spent reading texts they can read, not doing activities about reading. We need to take a more flexible, broader view of guided reading and look at it in the context of the Optimal Learning Model. The child is in charge and is holding the book; we teachers are checking to see whether the child is applying what we've been teaching.

I define guided reading (see *Reading Essentials*, p. 151) as any learning context in which the teacher guides one or more students through some aspect of the reading process: choosing books, making sense of text, decoding and defining words, reading fluently, monitoring comprehension, determining the author's purpose, and so on. *The teacher builds on students' strengths and supports and demonstrates whatever is necessary to move the child toward independence.* Independence is the end goal, not meeting in a group.

Likewise, in teaching writing, our end goal is to have students write independently and skillfully for real-world purposes and audiences as well as to use writing to think, problem-solve, communicate, record, and so on. Certainly, students do need to be able to write on demand, but the surest way to help them do that successfully is to spend most instructional and practice time on writing authentic texts and to provide some limited practice on writing to a prompt.

Make **Curriculum** Relevant, Interesting, and Challenging

What kind of thinkers do we want our students to become? If we want our students to use their intellect, we and they need to do more exploration and investigation, begin with a problem or question and seek answers, not write to a formula or learn reading from a scripted lesson, which is so demeaning to kids' intelligence and potential.

We teachers get tired, which can make us complacent. It seems easier to pull out the same units each year without questioning their suitability for this year's students. But we must always question why we're doing what we're doing and why these students need to know what we're teaching. We need to ask ourselves continually, *So what? What difference will it make?* Teaching something with more intention or finding out what students are really interested in is hard. It takes thought, effort, extra hours, but in the long run we save time, because our students are engaged and want to learn.

Teaching these days is too often about remediation and isolated skills instead of acceleration and challenging curriculum. Often, a deficit model dominates—find out what's wrong and fix it. We need to shift our thinking, to begin by building on children's strengths (they all have them!) and teaching them to become successful, independent learners. *What can they do? What do they know?* We can go from there.

Start with the big ideas. Anything we teach students in depth is more likely to be learned. By contrast, when we teach students lots of facts without showing how these facts connect to important concepts, there is little understanding and retention of these facts. We must return repeatedly to important topics and build on students' knowledge. It is only with a strong foundation that students will know enough to interpret ideas, present a coherent point of view, and be able to justify their opinions and findings.

"We must return repeatedly to important topics and build on students' knowledge. It is only with a strong foundation that students will know enough to interpret ideas, present a coherent point of view, and be able to justify their opinions and findings."

Connect Content to Students' Lives

In social studies and science, connect what you are teaching—even in a required text—with students' lives. Whole-class reading about colonial times out of a textbook and then asking students questions printed at the end of the chapter is not teaching; it is covering material. Plan how you can make the content relevant to your students. "What would it have been like for you if you had grown up in colonial times? What kinds of toys would you have had? How would you have dressed? What was family life like? Do you think everything about life today is an improvement? Why or why not?"

In one school where the required social studies curriculum in the primary grades included a study of communities, students were dutifully reading required texts and learning about the police force, firefighters and how a community operates. I encouraged them to start closer to home and engage students' hearts and minds through their

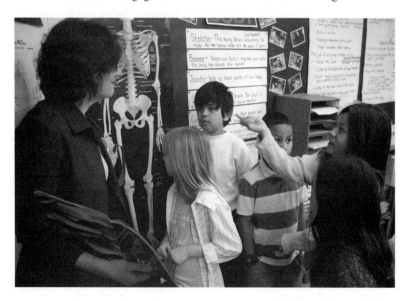

own school community. Who are the cafeteria workers? How do they determine the menus? What input do we want to give them? What are the custodians' responsibilities? How are the buses in the school district scheduled and maintained? How does water and heat come into the school building? The possibilities for authentic literacy activities are, as you can see, endless: interviews with school workers, invitations to school support staff to come to speak to the classroom, thank-you letters, posters to urge school pride in clean bathrooms and halls, recommendations about recess to the principal, a trip to the local water-processing plant, and much more.

Connect vital themes with sophisticated big questions and genuine inquiry on subjects that matter. What do students need to know and want to know? What must students be taught so they can understand the study? What can they discover on their own? How will you (and they) know what they have learned?

Teach for Understanding

"Many teachers who are required to use commercial literature anthologies and content textbooks are frustrated because not all students can read them."

In one of my reading residencies I was asked to demonstrate how to teach the required social studies text in a fifth-grade classroom. As a whole class, students had already read and discussed the first part of a chapter dealing with primary and secondary sources. Assessing what they knew before I continued, I asked, "What is a primary source? How are primary sources used? Why are they important?" Not one student could answer any of these questions, yet the plan had been to move ahead to the rest of the chapter. Sadly, this is typical. The material is "covered," but there is little understanding, and the "coverage" is useless.

To make the concept of primary sources relevant and interesting, I shared (with the help of the school's librarian) examples of primary sources connected to the local history of the southwestern city in which the school was located—newspaper clippings, brochures, historical accounts, letters, and other relevant resources. I asked, "How did your city get its name? Who settled here and why? Why is your local park named after so-and-so? How can we find this out?" We began to list primary sources that might help us, and once the students examined a few primary sources (following the Optimal Learning Model), they began to realize what a primary source was, how it might be useful, and how it differed from a secondary source. Most important, because they were interested and engaged in our work together, the learning was enduring. Now the social studies chapter could begin to make sense. Before, without a foundation of basic knowledge, most students were merely reading the words and wasting valuable time.

Teaching for understanding must be at the heart of all our instruction. By teaching for understanding, the idea, topic, or process must:

- Have enduring value beyond the classroom.
- Reside at the heart of the discipline and be encountered in context.
- Need to be uncovered.
- Engage students.

The following questions are some that probe for deep understanding:

- *What should we make of this?*
- *What are the causes or reasons?*
- *From whose point of view?*
- *What is this an instance of?*
- *How should this be qualified?*
- *So what? What is the significance?*

(Also see in *Conversations*, Routman, 2000, p. 472)

Use a Required Textbook as a Shared Read-Aloud

Many teachers who are required to use commercial literature anthologies and content textbooks are frustrated because not all students can read them. A frequent solution is for the teacher to read the stories or nonfiction texts aloud as the students track the print. From time to time the teacher asks some questions from the teacher's manual, but opportunities for responsive teaching, thinking aloud, and talking about the material are few and far between. Most important, the teacher often has no idea whether or not all students understand the text. Following along in a text does not mean reading with understanding.

Using the same literature selection or textbook as a shared read-aloud provides far more opportunities for relevant teaching, focused talk, and student engagement. (In a shared read-aloud, I am doing much of the reading aloud and thinking aloud and, occasionally, projecting an easy-to-read page or two, for students to read and think through together with a partner or two.) A shared read-aloud is purposeful; it is not just a communal reading of words. Reading along and talking along are effective techniques for increasing the amount of reading students do and their degree of understanding. This is also a great use of the required social studies or science text, which often is too difficult for most students to read easily.

Make **No Assumptions**

In a school where almost 90 percent of the students receive free or reduced-price breakfast and lunch, I am doing an interactive read-aloud in a second-grade classroom. (I am doing all the reading aloud and thinking aloud and, occasionally, stopping to give the children opportunities to talk about the text and to assess their understanding.) For this first meeting with the children, I have deliberately selected a marvelous nonfiction book, *Owen & Mzee: The True Story of a Remarkable Friendship*, by Isabella Hatkoff, Craig Hatkoff, and Dr. Paula Kahumbu, with photographs by Peter Greste (Scholastic Press, 2006). (The week prior to coming I had a planning meeting by phone with the classroom teacher and had asked about the children's interests; the teacher responded that they liked nonfiction books about animals.)

Owen & Mzee is the true story of a baby hippo named Owen who is washed away down river during the December 2004 tsunami in Southeast Asia, rescued, and brought to a sanctuary, where he and Mzee, a 130-year-old giant tortoise, become inseparable. This poignant, charming story speaks to the power of resilience and friendship. I have used it with students in grades 2 through 5 (as well as the equally marvelous sequel, *Owen & Mzee: The Language of Friendship*, Scholastic Press, 2007).

Choosing to use this challenging book in a second-grade classroom where most of the students come from low-income families and at least half are English language learners was deliberate. These students, like all students, need challenging, rich curriculum. As I began reading the story aloud, I stopped as I always do to explain what was happening in the story and what I was thinking. To check whether the children understood the story, I had them "turn and talk" about the most important things that had happened so far. When I called on several students to share, it became apparent that their unfamiliarity with basic vocabulary was impeding their comprehension. For example, they did not know what a flood was (the reason the baby hippo winds up in a strange place) or the meaning of *angry* (necessary to understand the hippo's behavior when strangers handle him during his rescue). Therefore, they could not understand what happened to the baby hippo and why. When I tried to explain *flood* by relating it to Hurricane Katrina, I found out none of them knew about that natural disaster. That shocked and saddened me. How could students not know about the greatest natural disaster in their lifetime? Later on, teachers told me the students had been "exposed" to Hurricane Katrina in first grade, but a year later, not one student could say anything about it. Exposure is not learning.

Had the students learned about it through personal connections and relevant curriculum, they could have applied that learning to a new context. These second graders looked like they were understanding, but they were not. They were merely behaving and being compliant.

Highlight Key Vocabulary

In general, students who do well in school have excellent vocabularies. In fact, having a rich vocabulary is one of the indicators of a well-educated person. As we just saw, students with meager vocabularies have difficulty understanding what they read and hear read aloud. They also are unable to interpret questions on high-stakes tests and follow written and oral directions.

While the surest way to increase one's vocabulary is through wide reading, direct teaching of vocabulary and strategies to figure out vocabulary is also necessary. According to the latest research on effective vocabulary instruction (Blachowicz et al., 2006):

- It takes place in a language- and word-rich environment, often referred to as "word consciousness."
- It includes intentional teaching of selected words, providing multiple types of information about the new word as well as opportunities for repeated exposure, use, and practice.
- It includes teaching generative elements of words and word-learning strategies in ways that give students the ability to learn new words independently.

We also need to explain words when we are reading, writing, and talking.

While doing a shared writing in a primary-grades classroom I realized that the students didn't understand common vocabulary. We were writing to the superintendent of schools asking her assistance in fixing the broken window on an outside classroom door. The glass had already been replaced a few times, and the children needed reassurance the problem would finally be fixed. "Does everyone know what a broken window is?" I asked. Not all did. Even after a verbal explanation, several students were still unclear until we drew a picture.

What impedes comprehension for English language learners is their limited vocabulary in their second language. While some English language learners look like they understand because they can read fluently, fluency cannot always be correlated with comprehension, especially for older readers. Let your students know that smart people ask what a word means when they don't know. Be sure to explain what words mean when you are talking, reading and writing aloud, and demonstrating.

Do what you can to make word study memorable. Kids love talking about and using interesting words. Rote memorization of words on lists doesn't work; neither does defining a word and never referring to it again. As with everything we learn and retain, vocabulary must be connected to something students know and can relate to, and new words need to be integrated into meaningful contexts.

Nevertheless, don't hesitate to use "big words." We teachers typically simplify the vocabulary we use with kids based on their age and socioeconomic status. In the second-grade classroom I mentioned earlier, teachers were simplifying the words they were using. In my teaching, I used and explained the words *eavesdropping, procedures,* and *rituals.* Students learned these words easily, and loved doing so.

Make It Smart to Ask Questions

Ask questions and seek responses in ways that encourage taking risks. Smart teachers make it "cool" for students to ask questions. I say something like this:

> *Smart people ask questions when they don't know the meaning of a word, when they don't understand something, when they're not sure what to do. If I don't know, we can try to find out together.*

When a student offers a response, even if it seems "off the wall," try to validate the student. To clarify responses, try prompts like:

- *Tell me what made you think that.*
- *Say more about that.*

- *What made you say that?*

- *How did you know that?* (This encourages metacognition— thinking about thinking.)

In shared writing, where we are helping shape children's language and thinking, we need to accept all responses that make some sense. Write down the students' exact words, knowing they can be revised later. Often the same students will later notice what doesn't make sense and offer revisions. Having their initial thoughts accepted seems to give them the confidence to change them.

Students feel smart when they learn and can apply new concepts and vocabulary and ask intelligent questions. Desiree, a second grader struggling with reading and writing (see p. 20), emphasizes the new words she has learned from hearing *Owen and Mzee* read aloud and discussed, as shown below. She is now a proud learner.

Questions naturally arise when we are learning about something that matters to us. Spend a few days noticing how often your students raise thoughtful questions. If questions are few, think about why that might be the case. We teachers need to pay attention as well to how often *we* ask important questions in school and in our life beyond school. We have to be in an alert, learning mode—not on automatic pilot—to be the best teachers. We need to nourish our own intellects and imaginations in order to guide our students with maximum energy and authority. We need to make curiosity and smart questioning essential to teaching and learning.

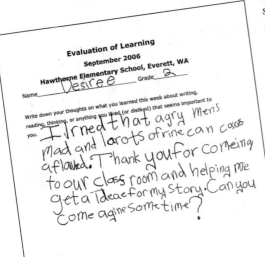

Evaluation of Learning
September 2006
Hawthorne Elementary School, Everett, WA

Name _Desiree_ Grade _2_

Write down your thoughts on what you learned this week about writing, reading, thinking, or anything you liked (or disliked) that seems important to you.

I lrned that agry mens mad and larots of rine can caes a flowd. Thank you for comeing to our class room and helping me get a Ideae for my story. Can you come agine some time?

It is puzzling that scores would drop for older students if fourth graders can truly read with understanding. One postulated reason is that there has been NO emphasis on reading help above grade 3 for a decade."

—RICHARD ALLINGTON,
NOTED EDUCATOR AND
RESEARCHER

CHAPTER 5

Embed Assessment in All Teaching

EFFECTIVE TEACHING IS SEAMLESS—a good teacher moves fluidly between teaching and assessing, explanation and response, demonstration and practice, everything happening in one uninterrupted motion. Even new teachers can embed assessment in their instruction from their earliest days in the classroom, so that it quickly becomes a habit. To succeed, teachers have to develop a mindset that views assessment not as an end product but as a vital, interactive part of responsive, effective teaching. Assessing *is* teaching.

Nevertheless, embedding assessment is a challenge because there is no script. As smart and thoughtful teachers, we have to listen, observe, note, rethink, and be willing to change directions—all while in the act of teaching. We have to be systematic but remain flexible and open. We have to be able to give immediate and specific feedback that is useful for improving student learning and work. We have to pay attention to the learners in front of us. It is this ability to think on one's feet that elevates teaching to a profession and craft. (The preceding statements are equally true for effective administrators.)

> " *Constant minute-by-minute assessment is what allows me to look at a particular child and envision the next possibility. In my mind, assessment is the driving decision-making force for all I do as a teacher.*"
>
> —TERRI S. THOMPSON, GRADE ONE TEACHER

Teach **Responsively**

I recently observed an outstanding teacher. The quality of her instruction was superb, as were her students' engagement, quality of work, and ability to problem-solve. If I had to name one factor that distinguished her effective teaching, it would be her interwoven assessment, most of which occurred as a result of responsive teaching.

By *responsive* teaching (as opposed to "telling" teaching, where the teacher tells the answer), I mean using mostly guided questioning and conversation to find out what students know and understand before, during, and after a lesson. The most effective teachers ask higher-level questions that prompt their students to engage actively in reading, writing, and responding. Reliance on "telling" is not beneficial to students' reading achievement (Taylor et al., 2002).

I have found the best way to use ongoing assessment to modify my instruction is to probe continually with questions. The answers I receive from the students reveal what students are learning, where they are confused, what I need to teach them, and what further demonstrations, resources, or strategies may be needed. This is very different from lecture-style presentations with the-teacher-as-expert in command. When we teach responsively we:

- Listen actively (in an attempt to understand what students are trying to say).

- Validate all responses (to accept students and encourage further response and risk taking).

- Seek to clarify thinking through specific, nonthreatening questions (to clear up confusions and prompt students to rethink and perhaps revise their responses).

- Encourage fuller and more thoughtful responses (by rephrasing what they have said in a manner that validates and even elevates their response and yet nudges them to think more deeply, and to justify their thinking).

- Try not to repeat what students have said (to show respect for the students and to encourage them to listen to one another, not just us).

In responsive teaching, skillful questioning sheds light on students' thinking and prods students to say how they know what they know.

Examples of such questions include but are not limited to:

- *How did you know that? What did you do to figure that out?*

- *Say more about that. What are you thinking?*

- *What did you notice? Why does that seem important?*

- *Why do you think thus-and-so?*

Responsive teaching is not the same as interactive teaching. In interactive teaching, we ensure a give-and-take in the conversation, which may or may not impact understanding and achievement. In responsive teaching we are intentionally interactive for specific purposes—to explore students' thinking, help them understand and explain their thinking, and nudge them to a higher level of understanding. When we teach responsively, we are teaching students to be metacognitive, which simply means to think about their thinking. We teach responsively as we check for understanding, hold scaffolded conversations (see pages 58 and 93), and guide collaborative small-group work. And, of course, we use what we learn from responsive teaching to make needed adjustments in our instruction before, during, and after teaching.

Provide Useful Feedback

To learn a task well, our students need constructive feedback. Partly because of the pressure we are under as teachers and administrators to "cover" the curriculum and teach the ever proliferating standards, we teach more and give less and less feedback to students. Useful feedback is necessary for them to do the quality work we expect. Also, when learners trust and respect the person giving the feedback, they are more likely to accept and apply that feedback. One of the most effective, efficient ways to give helpful feedback is through responsive teaching when checking for understanding.

Feedback is not praise ("*good job*") or advice ("*try harder*"). It is information students can use to improve the quality of their work. Feedback includes the following qualities (Wiggins, 2006). Some oral language examples are included. (The oral language examples are mine.)

- **It is specific to the task.** (*I saw you rereading several times as you were editing. That's what good editors do to be sure they've made all necessary corrections.*)

- **It is descriptive.** (*When you come across a word you don't know the meaning of, try reading the sentence before and after that word to help you figure out the word's meaning.*)

- **It uses language and concepts the student can handle and understand.** (*When you write your letter, be sure to make it sound* *like you, make your words clear and interesting for the reader, and let the reader know exactly what you want from her.)*

- **It states what the student did well and what the student needs to do or do better.** *(You're choosing fiction books you can read and understand pretty well. You can say what the main character is doing. Now, you want to slow down your reading a bit and reread in places to be sure you understand why the character is behaving and changing the way he is.)*

- **It is ongoing—it occurs before, during, and after learning.**

- **It includes demonstrations.** *(Let me show you how to do that.)*

- **It may include shared experiences as a way to try again.** *(I noticed that many of you are having difficulty figuring out the problem. Let's work it through together.)*

- **It provides step-by-step help, as needed.** *(Let me help you organize this piece. If we move this sentence here and add a transition here, your meaning will be clearer. Now, let's hear how it sounds and see what we need to add next.)*

Ultimately we want our students to be able to give themselves the feedback they need to move ahead independently. If we teach them how to evaluate their own learning and work, they are more likely to become self-motivated, independent learners. Even young students are able to do that.

Focus on the Students:
Begin with Assessment

I check in with students as they begin their work, assess how they are doing, and provide support, as needed.

No matter what and where I teach, I always start with assessment and modify instruction based on that assessment. In order to teach effectively, I must first know what knowledge students have or lack. So I ask them: *What do good writers do? How do you choose books to read? What do you know about the history of your city?* and so on. Most often, I chart students' responses so we can go back to them, add to them, and revise them as our understandings about a topic, idea, or process develops.

I accept all student verbal responses, which honors all learners. And as long as a response mostly makes sense, I write it on the chart exactly as the student expresses it. This lets students know that I respect their thinking and it saves time (since I don't have to look for a "better" response from another student). If a response seems confusing, I might say, *Tell me more about that,* or, *I'm not sure I understand what you're saying. Please say that again.* I can always "fix up" the responses later; I want all students to feel comfortable from the start to take a risk and share what they know and don't know.

Once I have a sense of what students know or don't know, I determine what basics I must teach and what resources I must provide before they can learn with understanding. Then, as we continue learning together through demonstrations, immersion, practice (always following the Optimal Learning Model), I reassess their growing knowledge, and we add that knowledge to our chart. (See chart at left for one example.)

Beginning with assessment lets me teach the unique individuals in front of me, not just a mandated curriculum. Here's how it plays out:

- What do students know?

- What do I need to teach them?

- What resources will I need beyond what I have already gathered?

- What background do I need to provide?

- What adjustments do I need to make and what supports do I need to provide for English language learners, special education students, and other special-needs learners?

When I go into classrooms (or coach principals about what to look for in their teachers' classrooms), I also start by talking with students first and looking at the work students are doing. The checklist below is a self-assessment guide for improving instruction and learning.

This chart shows how I first find out what students know about good writing so I know what to teach them. Notice how these writers are focused on correctness. After demonstrations that focused on meaning and audience and purpose, students' knowledge and writing quality grew.

WHAT TO LOOK FOR: FOCUS ON THE STUDENTS

- How self-directed are the students? Do they self-monitor, self-direct, and self-evaluate? Do they know how and when to seek help?

- Do the students know and understand the expectations for the task(s)? Are the task(s) relevant, meaningful, and appropriate? Are the expectations high enough?

- Can the students tell you why they're doing what they're doing? Do they understand and value the purpose of what they are engaged in? Can they name the audience their work is intended for?

- Are the students focused on high-level comprehension and strategies that promote deep thinking, such as summarizing, inferring, and analyzing? How much time are they spending

continues

WHAT TO LOOK FOR, *continued*

learning or practicing at the skills-in-isolation level? Can they apply their learning to new contexts?

- Are the students engaged in learning? What do you notice about pacing, interest, time management, organization, dedication to the task?

- Are the students assuming increasing responsibility for the task(s)? Who is doing most of the work? Do students have the necessary tools, strategies, and understanding to do the work?

- Are there lots of opportunities for meaningful talk and interaction? Are there opportunities for partner work and small-group work as well as whole-class and independent work?

- Are the students taking pride in their work? Are their ideas, revisions, handwriting, spelling, punctuation, and grammar excellent?

Examine Student Work

One of the ways we can know whether or not our students are learning more and learning at the highest levels they are capable of is to look at student work. The catch is that we have to know, in depth, what constitutes writing effectively, comprehending a text, explaining problem-solving in math, and so on. Without that solid knowledge accompanied by sufficiently high enough expectations, our judgments are superficial:

we merely "do" assessment, expending a lot of unnecessary time and energy. Whether or not teaching and student learning improve in worthwhile ways depends on our vision and depth of understanding. Examining student work as a grade-level or vertical team or with a partner, coach, or your principal will help you obtain a more objective and complete picture. The following chart lists some helpful guidelines.

GUIDELINES FOR LOOKING AT STUDENT WORK

- What do you notice (for example, about the content, organization, conventions)?

- What connections do you see to what was demonstrated and taught?

- How can you tell students picked up on (or didn't pick up on) what was taught?

- What have students done that shows they have met the expectations that were set?

- How do (or don't) students demonstrate that they have checked the work, rethought aspects of it, and taken full responsibility for the task?

- What is your evidence that students engaged (or did not engage) in the work?

- How can you tell if the work is the students' best effort? Is the work excellent? Mediocre? How do you know? What are your criteria for evaluation? Are these criteria reasonable?

- What evidence do you have that students have learned?

Rethink **Grouping Structures** in Reading

I have decided to address grouping within this assessment chapter because it is at once a powerful forum for both instruction *and* assessment. Working with students in small groups is an effective way to constantly assess how students are progressing and what they need to move forward. The big caveat I'll throw in, however, is that grouping is a means to an end, and as such, student groups must not be seen as something fixed for any significant span of time. The "end" is independent, self-monitoring, and self-sustaining readers. Teachers need to have this same end goal in mind for *all* student groups.

Grouping for instruction remains a controversial issue to which we need to apply research and common sense. A troubling trend is a return to ability grouping in the intermediate grades, sometimes called "walk to reading" because students leave their home classroom. One of the problems I have with that whole-class teaching scenario is that low-performing students are deprived of the benefits of thinking and discussing with higher-performing peers. Research confirms that, basically, homogenous grouping is not good for kids except when they are nonreaders—that is, when their reading skills are just beginning to develop. At the same time, common sense tells us that there are times when homogenous grouping is the best way to go. However, too often, students remain in a "low" reading group for the year and feel the sting of not measuring up. Even though teachers talk a lot about flexible groups, that flexibility is far too often in name only. We need to assess—and reassess continually—what grouping is most helpful for students to become confident, independent readers.

Also, make sure you have some way to assess what your students are accomplishing when you are working with small groups or conferring with students. One of the challenges with guided reading groups is that most of the students are on their own for long periods of time each day. Many "centers" in classrooms just keep kids busy, and, often, teachers do not check on what students have learned. Make sure that the independent work students are doing in any subject area is worthwhile, easy to assess, and that it is leading students to become more proficient, confident, and independent as readers, writers, and thinkers, and problem solvers.

"We need to assess—and reassess continually—what grouping is most helpful for students to become confident, independent readers."

Rely on Essential Grouping

In grades 1 and 2, or in any grade that includes developing readers, I do group by reading ability so I can teach students the basic skills and strategies they need to read independently: one-to-one matching, recognizing basic words on sight, solving words, reading with fluency, figuring out vocabulary, and comprehending what the words and sentences mean. Still, time spent in these groups is brief, between ten and twenty minutes. Much more reading instruction occurs during teacher think-alouds, shared reading experiences, and one-on-one conferences. And it is only through a great deal of independent reading of meaningful texts that students become readers. Any group work is always a means to an end, not the main goal.

Meet with Skills Groups as Necessary

Once students are readers, I don't use homogeneous grouping. Because I am conducting daily one-on-one reading conferences during the daily thirty to sixty minutes of independent reading, it is not a good use of my or the students' time to hear them whisper-read and read aloud in a group.

However, based on what I notice during my ongoing assessment—mostly in informal reading conferences—I may call a small group together (once or several times) to teach them specific strategies, such as how to figure out multisyllable words, discover the meaning of words they don't known, understand character motivation, or become familiar with how nonfiction texts work. I also do this with the whole class if I notice large numbers of students have the same need.

To avoid stigmatizing students as I call up a group, I say something like this:

> *If you need some help in figuring out multisyllable words when you're reading on your own, come on up. I'm going to show you some strategies for how to do that so when you come to an unknown word you'll know how to figure it out.*

Most of the students who need help know it and come up on their own. However, if they don't, I say something like, "Nathan, come on up and join us. I know this will be helpful for you." I've never had a student refuse that invitation, in part because all students welcome extra attention and they know they may learn something. Very often a student or two who doesn't need the help wants to join the group, and I always welcome that opportunity to add their greater expertise to the mix.

My best advice is to use common sense. One excellent, conscientious third-grade teacher abandoned all grouping for reading believing that it was always wrong to group students by ability. She wore herself out trying to teach everything, one student at a time. Only when she added small groups as described above to her daily reading conferences did she feel she was meeting the needs of all her students.

Value and Employ **Multiple Assessments**

In our test-obsessed culture, we must return sanity to classroom teaching. Formative, ongoing assessments—by teachers and students based on daily work—need to be the mainstay. **Formative assessments** are the most accurate indications of what a student can do and where instruction needs to be modified. Some examples of formative assessment are anecdotal records, observations during class discussions, quick-writes, responses to reading, explanations of thinking, teacher-constructed quizzes, conferences, rubrics, and self-assessments. Summative assessments take place periodically and are standardized—district and state tests, for example. Combined with formative assessments, summative assessments can help improve instruction and learning. By themselves, summative assessments do not provide a comprehensive picture of a child's achievement.

Real caution is needed here. Scores from the National Association of Educational Progress (NAEP) (U.S. Department of Education, 2004), also known as The Nation's Report Card, indicate that grade 8 and grade 12 reading scores are dropping while grade 4 scores have largely remained steady since about 2002. It is puzzling that scores would drop for older students if fourth graders can truly read with understanding. One postulated reason is that there has been "NO emphasis on reading help above grade 3 for a decade" (Allington, 2007). Meanwhile grade point averages and state scores are increasing. What could account for this? The pressure is so great to raise test scores that many states lower standards to make it look like more students are achieving. In fact, "not a single state sets their reading proficiency as high as the national test" and only a couple of states have standards that exceed the NAEP's.

For this standardized school assessment, all kindergarten students were given an oral prompt: "Write about a fun time in the snow."

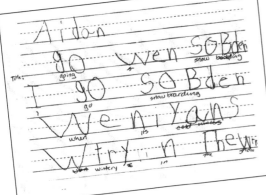

Going Snowboarding
I go snowboarding
when it's
wintery in the snow

Collect and Analyze Your Assessment Data to Improve Instruction

Looking at data is only valuable if we teachers and administrators are knowledgeable. I have found this to be especially true with writing and have advised administrators to delay having their staff look at student writing samples until they all know what to look for. Otherwise, lots of time may be spent overvaluing conventions or other writing qualities simply because we don't know what effective student writing looks like.

To attain high achievement school- and districtwide, it is important to know what effective practices and student work look like across grade levels. At one school, seeing what typical writing looked like midyear in kindergarten (see writing at left) pushed intermediate-grade teachers to expect much more from their students.

Look at data as a leadership team or whole staff, by specific grade levels and across grade levels. Look at typical writing as well as the writ-

These are fifth- and sixth-grade students working in small, self-directed groups. (There were six groups like this going on at the same time.) Students are reading and talking through a nonfiction article together while one student serves as a scribe to record the most important ideas. In this way, the teacher has a record of each group's thinking while she either joins one group or does roving conferences.

ing of struggling and gifted students. What strengths do you notice? Where are the weaknesses? Are expectations high enough? What goals need to be set? What interventions are needed?

When Ardmore Elementary School in Bellevue, Washington recently looked at schoolwide reading achievement, it was apparent that too many third graders were still having difficulty reading, especially when it came to solving words. After whole-school professional conversations, the principal and staff decided to reallocate their school support staff, providing extra instruction to the three or four struggling readers in each grade 1 classroom. Until the whole staff carefully examined the data, the first-grade teachers, who were all very knowledgeable and dedicated teachers of reading, were becoming frustrated trying to "fit it all in"— daily guided practice, additional word work, more publishing of kids' writing, and reading more texts. Because of the resulting additional in-classroom support, these teachers, who had always been committed to meeting the needs of all their readers, could finally do so.

How do you know all *your students understand what they read?* You can't tell in typical whole-class or small-group instruction. Once one student answers "correctly," we don't know if the others "got it." Make sure you know through hard data. For example, when I conduct a small guided reading group, I may have the students read a few pages silently and answer a question in a small spiral notebook. I can immediately tell who is ready to move on and who needs explicit instruction. When students work in self-directed small groups for math, social studies, or reading response, I make sure I have a written record of each group's thinking so I know what they have understood and where more demonstrations and support are needed. (See the work of two groups, p. 24, as an example.)

On a schoolwide level, checking date requires collaboration, collegial trust, and an unwavering commitment by the principal and staff. For example, as a principal in Maryland, Thommie Piercy scheduled time and a floating substitute each marking period to have face-to-face conversations with every teacher about the reading progress of each of the schools' 850 students. With accountability focused at the student level and shared among the principal, teacher, team, and whole school, students' high achievement gains in reading were sustained.

Continuously Check for Understanding

Students can look like they are understanding and still not comprehend. That is, they look straight at us, appear to be listening, and are well behaved. But compliant behavior cannot be equated with student engagement and learning.

Some ways to check for understanding are to monitor student responses in the following learning situations:

- Think-pair-share.
- Turn-and-talk.
- Small-group thinking recorded by a scribe.
- Interactive read-aloud.
- Shared writing.
- Self-directed literature conversations.
- Conferences (public and one-on-one).

When a lesson goes badly and I don't get the results I anticipated, I rethink and regroup: *What didn't I do? What do I need to do? What demonstrations, information, practice, resources, do I need to add to ensure students will be successful?* My mindset is always that the students are fine as long as I do enough frontloading, I'm explicit enough, the lesson is relevant to them, and they understand its purpose. (Also see Chapters 4 and 6).

Apply a Useful Framework

In my experience, the most effective teachers are aware at every moment how well their students understand and adjust their teaching as necessary to ensure that their students *do* understand. You can use the framework as shown below as a guide to help you check for understanding before, during, and after every lesson. More than that, make sure you also teach your students how to continually assess and improve their own learning practices.

ONGOING ASSESSMENT:

A FRAMEWORK FOR CHECKING FOR UNDERSTANDING

Helping Students Become Independent Learners

- **Make sure students know, understand, and can state the purpose of the instruction, task, activity.**
  - Ask, *Why are we doing what we're doing* (as a whole class, in small groups, with a partner, individually)?
  - State, write down, and project goals and objectives for and with students. (Later, check off what was accomplished during your celebration of what has been learned.)

- **Have students try out what you have been demonstrating.**
  - Implement shared and guided experiences (as a whole

ONGOING ASSESSMENT, *continued*

class, in small groups, with a partner) before expecting students to succeed on their own.

- Provide opportunities for scaffolded conversations.
- Provide and demonstrate how to use supportive resources.
- Provide opportunities for differentiated instruction, learning, and follow-up activities.

■ **Check (through oral statements or a written plan) that students are clear about what they are expected to do.**

- Have students show their plan—brainstorming, outlining.
- Have one or two students say back to you what students are expected to do.
  - If she or he cannot, have another student publicly make that statement as the first student listens carefully.
  - Have original student restate expectations.
  - Repeat if necessary.
  - Create a rubric together (based on demonstrations, shared writing, district and state requirements and standards).
- For English language learners, write down expectations (for example, a language goal, a reading goal, and a writing goal) so students have a visual reference. Later, check off what has been accomplished.

■ **Find out what students know before, during, and after the lesson.**
What's your evidence that students know such-and-such?

- Ask questions that encourage response (so you hear all the voices and scaffold students' thinking). For example:
  - *Who sees something they know?* vs. *Who can spell (a specific word?)*
  - *What did you notice?* Use students' responses to gauge their understanding and guide your teaching, immersing, questioning, demonstrating, opportunities for talk. (You can also chart their responses and use the chart later to set expectations and as a reference for self-evaluation.)
  - *How did you know that?*
- Show students their growing learning so they understand their knowledge is increasing. (Make visual aids, charts, lists. Add on to them/revise them as students learn more.)
- Make learning comprehensible for English language learners through Total Physical Response, such as hand gestures and dramatizations.

continues

ONGOING ASSESSMENT, *continued*

- Use turn-and-talk and partner and small-group discussions.
- Have small self-directed groups appoint a scribe to record their thinking, and/or walk about as groups are working and observe and take notes. Have groups report how the group activity went.
- Note and build in additional support and supplementary materials/scaffolds for special needs learners (gifted, ELLs, struggling).

■ **Provide useful feedback to students.**
  - Confer with students regularly (roving check-ins, whole-class shares, one-on-one conferences).
  - Welcome and affirm approximations that show reasoned thinking.
  - Use language that is specific to the task. See pages 73–74 for some examples. (Avoid negative terms.)

■ **Collect and analyze evidence and data that students are progressing and meeting district benchmarks and state standards.**
  - Implement and analyze formative assessments, such as running records, informal reading and writing conferences, daily work samples, portfolios, self-assessments, worksheets created from class-authored shared writings.
  - Implement and analyze summative assessments, such as school and district assessments, state tests.
  - Use and value student self-assessments and self-evaluations.
  - Meet with grade-level and whole-school colleagues and—based on student work—notice what and where students are achieving well and where more attention is needed.
  - Use your data and analysis to set new goals and then plan for areas for intervention, professional development, and instructional changes.

■ **Observe and document whether students are applying their learning to new contexts.** Gather evidence that demonstrates that students can and do:
  - Transfer their learning and strategies across the curriculum.
  - Problem-solve independently to make meaning.
  - Explain their thinking.
  - Locate and use appropriate resources and strategies and apply them to unfamiliar contexts.

ONGOING ASSESSMENT, *continued*

- Self-monitor, self-correct, self-check their work.
    - Use resources (such as word walls, classroom charts, manipulatives, and the library) to effectively make meaning.
    - Reread a text (in reading and writing).
    - Check with an excellent model and ask, *Is it right? How do I know? What can I do to find out?*
    - Edit independently.
- If students do not apply what has been demonstrated and practiced, go back to the Optimal Learning Model. Focus on demonstration and shared demonstration before releasing responsibility for the task(s) to students.

- **Notice and document if students are choosing to go on learning. Observe if students independently:**
    - Choose to read/write more on the same or a related topic.
    - Monitor and improve the quality of their own work.
    - Set their own goals for continued learning.
    - Problem-solve confidently in new contexts, applying learned strategies.
    - Mentor and teach others.

Although it's not easy to do, try thinking of assessment as part of all teaching and not separate from it. You may need to suspend ingrained beliefs and practices, but it will be worth the challenge and the change. You and your students will interact more meaningfully, achieve more in less time, and experience greater engagement and enjoyment.

"I've now become much more specific about my feedback to students. I've been writing down the smart thinking and strategies students use when we confer . . ."

—Elizabeth Kappler, third-grade teacher

CHAPTER 6

Teach for Independent,
Self-Directed Learners

TAKE A CLOSE LOOK AT YOUR TEACHING. Who's doing most of the
thinking and the work?

In a first-grade classroom, the teacher is leading a guided reading group of four struggling readers, and she's doing almost all the
problem solving—supplying words, telling what the story is about,
ensuring students are following along. When students go back to their
seats to practice what they have just read, they are unable to do so
independently and quickly lose interest. Noticing their off-task behavior, the teacher has to abandon her present reading group and
rephrase what the students in the earlier group are to do. Their "practice" has become a time of frustration for the whole class.

Teachers often tell me they are surprised when their students
don't fare well on high-stakes writing tests because these same students are doing well in writing in the classroom. However, in large
part, these teachers are pointing out to students when and what they
need to fix up and often doing much of the revising and editing for
them. Naturally, on a test with no one there to advise them that they
need better organization or correct conventions, their efforts are dis-
appointing. Our students don't automatically check and revise their
writing just because they're working independently or taking a test.

> *My brain hurts from
> all the thinking because I
> never think, but now I'm get-
> ting smarter. We all cooper-
> ated and were not bossy. Now
> I feel good about learning. I
> feel confident, brave, smarter.
> My brain feels bigger. I have
> knowledge in my head. I feel
> great."*
>
> —NATALIE, A
> STRUGGLING THIRD
> GRADER'S SELF-
> EVALUATION AFTER A
> READING RESIDENCY

We need to teach them to monitor and evaluate their own work and direct their own revision process right from the start. Even kindergartners can learn to reread their writing to see whether it makes sense and add a missing word if necessary.

Students who can apply what has been learned in one context to new learning situations do well in school, on tests, and ultimately on the job. I believe the end goal of education must be to teach our students to be independent problem solvers who direct their own learning and set new, worthwhile goals.

Evaluation of Learning
January 2006   **WA**
Elementary School,

Name *Natalie C*   Grade *3rd*

Write down your thoughts on what you learned this week about reading, thinking, working in a group, or anything else that seems important to you.

My head hurts from all the thinking. Because I never think but now I'm getting smarter. We all cowperated and were not bossy. Now I feel good about learning. I feel conphdent, braver, smarter. My brain feels biger. I have nalege in my head I feel great!

Natalie's self-evaluation
(see epigraph, p. 87).

Apply the **Optimal Learning Model**

"I believe the end goal of education must be to teach our students to be independent problem solvers who direct their own learning and set new, worthwhile goals."

Learner independence is achieved through sufficient and effective demonstrations, many shared experiences, and ample guided and independent practice. See the Optimal Learning Model chart on the inside front cover. Becoming independent also depends on learning from a knowledgeable, trustworthy source and having the task or text presented as a meaningful whole before breaking it down into its parts. For the task or text to be meaningful, the learner first has to have enough background knowledge and vocabulary to understand it. All of this is as true for middle and high school learners as it is for elementary students.

Here's a personal story. In creating the *Transforming Our Teaching* projects (Routman 2008) showing educators what the whole of effective teaching looks like and sounds like, I needed to learn how to transfer video clips from a video camera to my Macintosh computer. Being a self-acknowledged technophobe with limited skills in this venue, I sought help from Rhett, one of Apple's local "MacGeniuses." Having no background to understand what my patient tutor was showing me, I took detailed notes listing the step-by-step procedures, beginning with, "Turn on the camera." Once Rhett left, I looked at my notes, turned on the video camera, and froze. I had no idea what to do next and no background to understand what I had written down. I was so focused on getting each step recorded in sequence that I never understood how these steps or parts connected to the whole process.

When I met with Rhett the following week, we began again. I explained to him that I could not even begin to apply what he had shown me the previous week. He replied, "It's like you're standing on the roof of

THE OPTIMAL LEARNING MODEL

Teaching and Learning Contexts	Who Holds Book/Pen	Degree of Explicitness/Support
Celebration & Assessment Are Embedded		
Reading and Writing Aloud	**Teacher**/Student	**Demonstration**
Shared Reading and Writing Scaffolded Conversations	**Teacher**/Student	**Shared Demonstration**
gradual handover of responsibility		
Guided Reading Literature Conversations Reading/Writing Conferences	**Student**/Teacher	**Guided Practice**
Independent Reading/Writing	**Student**/Teacher	**Independent Practice**
Celebration & Assessment Are Embedded		

a building with a shaky foundation." It was an apt description. Without the basics, the best I could do was rotely follow procedures.

For this meeting, I set aside step-by-step thinking and began to look at the whole. I took no notes. Instead, I tried hard to watch carefully what Rhett was doing, listen to his explanations, and attempt to understand the technical operations and the reasons for doing them. I still didn't know enough to ask intelligent questions. But in this meeting, I not only observed what he was doing but also requested he not leave until we had gone through the procedures together. I would need this "We do it" experience several more times before I had enough confidence and know-how to try out the process with Rhett's guidance—that is, with him by my side but with me now taking the lead. Eventually I could transfer a video clip from my camera to my computer, but just barely. I never got beyond the procedural level of following steps. More important, I never truly "learned" the activity, because I am unable to do it today. Like many of our students, I was "exposed" to the activity; the material was "covered." I had a competent and patient teacher, but too few shared demonstrations—along with insufficient practice, background knowledge, and understanding—left me unable to apply what I was being taught.

My discomfort and lack of confidence in this new learning situation brought home once again the point that for learning to be successful, the learner must:

- Need and want to learn something (or, at a minimum, see the purpose for the lesson).

- Have sufficient background knowledge, vocabulary, and skills to understand the task or text and ask intelligent questions (or receive the necessary background before attempting the task or text).

- Admire and trust the teacher or expert.

- Be shown how to do it (through demonstration, explanation, reading about it, viewing it).

- Have repeated opportunities to try out the task or process, with much support and hand-holding (shared experiences).

- Be given ample time for guided and independent practice with helpful feedback.

- Learn enough strategies to begin to problem solve independently.

- Eventually be able to apply the learning to new contexts.

A significant classroom-based insight is that the learner can't ask questions without a basic knowledge of the subject. This is why so many of our struggling learners are silent. They don't know enough about the subject at hand to know what their questions are, and they remain on shaky ground. I was unable ask Rhett intelligent questions because I lacked even a rudimentary understanding of what we were undertaking.

Also, most importantly, students need to spend most of their time "doing." Without opportunities and sustained time to practice, the best lesson can go nowhere. It is while practicing that you learn what you don't know and what your questions are. To teach successfully, we need to follow the Optimal Learning Model, following our demonstrations with lots of time and opportunity for guided talk, collaboration, practice, and coaching.

Do Lots of Frontloading

The better job we do preparing students to do a task (frontloading), the more independently students—even our youngest ones—are able to work and problem solve and produce better-quality work. We cannot expect them to succeed without adequate frontloading.

Working with a class of twenty-three kindergartners (see the related discussion on pp. 25–27), many of whom were English language learners, all are able to work independently writing stories about their lives. Even though the task is new to them, the frontloading we did together makes their accomplishments possible. They hear lots of stories read aloud, see and examine published books written by other kindergartners, observe me think aloud and write my own story about my cat Norman, hear and participate in public scaffolded conversations before writing, and have a quick (roving) conference with me as they are writing.

The following factors, all part of the Optimal Learning Model, also make their success possible:

- The task is engaging and makes sense.

- Expectations are clear.

- Demonstrations are plentiful and relevant (shared writing, teacher thinking aloud and writing, public scaffolded conversations, exemplary work from former students).

- Opportunities to practice—try out and apply what has been demonstrated and scaffolded—are frequent and sustained.

- Supportive resources (peers, word walls, dictionaries, charts, classroom library) are available, accessible, and easy to use.

- Helpful feedback is ongoing.

- The outcome is known (celebrating, publishing, teaching, evaluating).

Capitalize on Shared Experiences

When we follow the Optimal Learning Model by building on students' strengths and releasing responsibility to students when they are ready to apply what we've been teaching, students have immediate success. Think of the OLM as, *I do it, We do it, We do it, We do it, You do it.*

Shared experiences (*We do it*) often make the critical difference between a student's (or a teacher's) ultimate success or frustration. Teachers often say they don't have time for shared experiences because of curriculum demands, limited time, and testing pressures. Typically, teachers move from "I do it" to "Now you do it" with resulting frustration and failure for many students. Many teachers in the intermediate grades as well as in middle school and high school believe that such "hand-holding" will slow things down. Just the opposite. Sometimes you have to "slow down to hurry up." For many middle school readers, who continue to struggle after years of failure, the OLM and its focus on shared and scaffolded experiences is the framework for successful intervention in all content areas.

Shared literacy experiences—in which the in-charge expert holds the pen or book while soliciting and shaping responses from students—provide the scaffolding and hand-holding learners need before they can become independent. "We do it" can take several forms:

- Teacher with student(s).

- Teacher with teacher.

- Students with students (small groups).

- Partner work.

| This is a demonstration for the teacher and students before expecting them to attempt a task, with support.

The latter two groupings require that demonstration and practice have already taken place. Most often, I demonstrate with the whole class gathered together and looking on. For example, before I release students to partner-read or read together in a small group:

- I demonstrate (perhaps more than once) what that looks like and sounds like as I direct a student or group of students.

- I lead another demonstration in which students actively participate.

- Students try out the process with me at their side to coach them and give helpful feedback.

- I repeat as needed until several students or groups of students have demonstrated they are capable of undertaking the task with limited assistance.

Here's another example. In a fourth-grade classroom in which students were learning how to write research reports, small student groups wrote their final reports collaboratively. First, the teacher, Darcy Ballentine, demonstrated how to take notes and turn them into a cohesive paragraph. Next, using the same notes, she had students write another paragraph with her. Then small groups of three or four students (mixed abilities and genders) turned the rest of the notes into a report, with Darcy available to guide them through the process.

Our thinking was that the students would be most successful writing their final reports if they worked collaboratively: they were not yet ready to write individual reports that would match this quality. The process worked out well. The final published reports of each group were excellent, and eight of the twenty-one students in the class were rated advanced on the extended writing portion of the state's rigorous writing test (all but two of the remaining students received a proficient rating).

Embrace Scaffolded Conversations

By scaffolded conversations I mean focused talk that prompts students to think about and express ideas they might not generate on their own. In a scaffolded conversation, I am face-to-face with the child in a natural, give-and-take exchange. I concentrate on what the child is trying to say and focus my talk and questions there. Scaffolded conversations take place as part of celebrations, conferences, and content-area learning and:

- Build on the student's strengths.

- Extend what the child is attempting to do.

- Suggest language and ideas for the child to consider.

- Celebrate memorable language the child has employed.

Here I am having additional scaffolded conversations with a few students who are not quite ready to work independently.

While scaffolded conversations take place throughout the day and across the curriculum, most often I have these conversations publicly during writing time and tell the class something like this: *I am going to have a conversation with Michael. Even though it's about his writing, it's important for you to carefully listen, because you'll get ideas for your own writing.* Then I check for understanding: *OK, turn-and-talk to your partner. Tell each other the reason we're having these conversations.* If we want students to engage and apply what they learn from our demonstrations, we have to be sure they understand and value the purpose for them.

I used to quickly go around the classroom before students were about to write and ask each student to name their topic. Not surprisingly, much of the resulting writing was superficial, in keeping with my simple question. When I embraced "less is more" and had public, in-depth conversations with just one or two students about their topic and how they might develop it, the results were dramatic. Great detail, elaboration, and voice began to appear in students' writing (without my labeling those traits).

To capture students' ideas and unique language so that they (and I) can remember them, I jot them down on a sticky note, which the children then attach to their paper. Some teachers provide a small notebook (a commercial one or just pages stapled together) so all comments are collected in one place for each student. Writing down key words from the conversation:

- Lets the child (and other students) know that what has been expressed is noteworthy.

- Jogs the child's memory when he or she begins to write.

- Encourages other students to attempt similar ideas, organization, and language.

  - Reminds the teacher what was discussed, which can be helpful when celebrating and conferring.

  - Provides a record of the child's thinking.

I never omit scaffolded conversations, especially for our English language learners and struggling students. Saying the story or factual information—with our support—before they write it promotes higher-quality language, better organization of thinking and content, and greater possibilities for what the child can accomplish. See the OLM on the inside front cover and notice the area of scaffolded conversations.

Here are two children telling their stories before writing them out. They are also getting ideas from their peers.

Set Up the Learning Environment for Success

When a lesson goes badly, I ask myself, *What didn't I do that is causing the students not to be successful?* I never think, *What's wrong with these students?* I place the responsibility on me, where it belongs, because I know from years of experience that the kids are fine and will learn if I set up the learning environment so they can succeed.

I set up the learning environment for success by providing:

- The rationale for what we're about to undertake.

- Explicit demonstrations and explanations.

- Lots of shared experiences.

- Opportunities for negotiating the curriculum. (Students have some say in what we'll read and write about and how we'll read and write it.)

- Support and encouragement to all learners so they experience success. (This may mean my calling on a reticent student and doing some hand-holding.)

- Many opportunities for talking, predicting, listening, thinking, asking questions, giving input. (I often tell students, *I'm not looking for a right answer. I want your best thinking. You have something to say. Take your time.* And, *Smart people ask questions. There are no stupid questions. If you don't know what something means, ask.*)

- Ample time for guided practice.
- Ongoing feedback (nudging, raising expectations).
- Opportunities for evaluation and reflection.
- Celebration of small and big successes and contributions.

Monitor Your Own Teaching

Ask yourself these questions before expecting students to undertake a task or text on their own:

- Is what I am asking students to do helping them become smarter and more independent as thinkers and learners?
- Do students understand what they are to do? How do I know?
- Have I adequately prepared them for the task?
- Have I ensured that students have the necessary background knowledge before they attempt the task or text?
- Have I clearly demonstrated everything I want students to do?
- Have students engaged in sufficient shared demonstrations? How do I know?
- Have I provided appropriate resources and supports for all learners?
- Is most of students' time spent practicing and applying what they are learning?
- Have I built in enough assessments to inform and guide my instruction?
- Have I provided time for celebration?

Make **Management** Easy

I have included classroom management in this chapter on self-directed learners because students' ability to monitor their own behavior and activity is a result not only of our ongoing instruction and assessment but also of excellent, self-sustaining classroom management. Effective management is a partnership; it depends on collaboration. We show our students how learning is carried out, and they are responsible for doing so. Self-management and self-direction are important because the *practice* element of the Optimal Learning Model is essential. It doesn't matter how great our demonstrations and lessons are; without an expanse of time in which to practice the techniques and strategies we're teaching, students won't be able to apply them.

Teach with a Sense of Urgency

"Firmness and kindness are not mutually exclusive. I do not thank students for behaving. That is their job."

One of the best ways to keep students engaged (in which case classroom management becomes a nonissue) is to teach with a sense of urgency—that is, with the expectation that there is not a minute to lose, that every moment must be used for purposeful instruction, assessment, practice, coaching, and so on. I am constantly stunned at how much classroom time is wasted on administrative announcements, complex directions, lost attention, isolated exercises unrelated to a meaningful whole, and the school calendar. All of these and more take students off task and squander time meant for learning.

I find that if what I am teaching students is interesting, relevant, and comprehensible—and if I move at a steady pace, teach responsively, and ignore small distractions—students come along with me and stay focused on the lesson.

Be Direct, Firm, and Kind

Of course, we want our students to talk with one another in a respectful and intelligent manner, and we model that behavior for them by the way we talk to and treat our students, their families, and our colleagues. If students are to work and problem solve together productively, they have to learn and practice the language of respect. We can model how to be very direct and still be respectful.

Firmness and kindness are not mutually exclusive. I do not thank students for behaving. That is their job. A principal never thanked me for teaching each day, nor did I expect it. However, I might say, *When we were doing our shared reading today, I noticed everyone was following along with the text. That's great, because one of the ways you become a better reader is to read lots of texts.* Nor do I stop teaching and say, *I'm waiting for so-and-so to put look up here,* which wastes valuable time. Instead, I say something along these lines: *What we're doing today is important. Here's why we're doing what we're doing and why I need your attention. Okay, let's start again and have everyone with us.*

Once in a while, a student will deliberately test me—not pay attention and ignore the required task. Then I am very firm and say, sometimes publicly, *My job is to teach you. Your job is to learn.* Then I again ask the student to do what was previously requested.

Finally, very important, I try hard not to repeat what a student has said. Students learn that they need to listen to me and one another the first time, and this allows me more time for instruction.

Provide Choice Within Structure

We all do better when we have some choice in what we are being asked to do. A high school student told me that over the summer she was required to read three specific books on which she would be tested on the first day of school. Why not have students choose three books from a list of twenty and show their understanding by keeping a response log of their thinking? The objection I always hear is, "How will we know they really read the books?" My answer? Reading a log of a student's thinking, even in response to specific predetermined criteria, tells us much more about what that student has understood and imagined than a one-size-fits-all test.

Much of the choice I provide is choice within structure. That is, although I have determined the task, students have wide latitude in how they set up the classroom library, what writing topics they pick, what kind of research they do, and what books they read. Students must have lots of free choice in reading and writing if they are to become readers and writers. Most independent reading must be of books the students have chosen themselves and that are at a level they can read and understand. And at least one day a week students need to be able to choose their writing genre and topic. It's not anything goes, because that can produce lots of substandard writing. Again, I rely on choice within structure. That is, if they are going to write fiction or a play or create a magazine, either I have already taught them how to do that kind of writing or they prepare a written plan convincing me they know how to do it.

These fourth graders, on their own, used writing to seek help for victims of Hurricane Katrina.

Let Students Help You Determine Procedures and Behavior

Many rules are non-negotiable. However, how the people in the classroom will treat one another, how the classroom library will be organized, and even what will be posted on the bulletin boards can be decided in conjunction with students. One of the most effective ways to do this is through shared writing, in which you negotiate students' ideas

How to sharpen a pencil
how to prepare snack
How to choose a book to read
how to listen to a story
How to line up
how to do Wahoo reading
~~How to act in class~~
how to get your lunch in the lunchroom
How to play on the playground
How to put a book back when you're done with a
How to walk in the hall
How to act in classroom library
How to act when you're learning
... sit down in your chair
act in the bathroom
act in math
act in music
act in lunchroom
be a PE

This chart shows how we used shared writing to determine needed topics for a classroom book on procedures.

and suggestions but remain the final arbitrator and scribe. Make sure everything is worded in a positive way (*treat each other kindly* instead of *don't be mean*). Then post these procedures and ways of behaving in the classroom.

In Ginny Vale's fourth-grade classroom, we negotiate expected classroom behaviors at the start of the school year. We begin with a whole-class shared writing, move to self-directed, small-group work where students work together to improve the writing, and come together as a class to finalize our list. The final chart remains posted in the classroom all year. Students know they are expected to self-manage these behaviors, and they take the task seriously.

Create a Beautiful and Organized Environment

I am married to an architect and artist, so over the years I've become more sensitive to the interplay of space, color, room arrangement, and lighting. A beautiful, comfortable, well-thought-out space can impact our sense of well-being and our desire to learn and work. You and your students spend many hours each day in your classroom and in the school. Work together to make it as peaceful, organized, and pleasing as possible.

Here is a library corner in a kindergarten classroom.

Look around. Is there a homogenized look to classrooms, bulletin boards, and hallway displays, or do they reflect the uniqueness of your student body? Make sure posted work has correct conventions and shows pride in workmanship. Think about what kids find beautiful. They don't necessarily prefer commercially published, polished materials. They want to see themselves on the walls—their work, their ideas, their handwriting, even their photographs.

Make sure that what is posted and displayed in your classroom is worthy but also accessible. Does your library have a section that high-lights students' published work? Are these pieces treated as seriously as the commercially published books? Do books face out so students can see the covers easily?

"Make certain that the classroom library represents students' interests and needs and that it is the centerpiece of the classroom."

Have students help decide how the classroom library will be organized. Negotiate the various authors, topics, and genres to be represented and how they will be categorized. Classroom libraries work best when students share in the ownership of the library and have the chance to take the books home. Make certain that the classroom library represents students' interests and needs and that it is the centerpiece of the classroom. Encourage students to care for the library and volunteer for the many jobs necessary to keep it running smoothly, which also saves you time to do other tasks.

Keep Things Simple and Organized

The only way to work with small groups or confer with students one on one and still ensure that the other students are on task is to simplify our management procedures and organize our classroom so students can work without our assistance. Small things—dictionaries that are too sophisticated, writing paper that isn't appropriate for the task, storage areas that are difficult to reach—can get students off task.

Here's an example. While teaching in a first-grade classroom, I noticed that the procedures for getting paper for writing were so cumbersome—it had taken weeks of demonstrations and practice for students to learn which shelf to use to find the "right" kind of paper for each assignment—that a lot of time that could have been spent writing was still being used to re-teach and reinforce correct procedures.

Check yourself. Is most of students' time spent practicing and applying what you have been teaching, or is a disproportionate amount of time spent following your directions? Is most of your time spent putting up bulletin board displays, planning elaborate projects, and marking papers, or is most of your time spent thinking and reflecting about teaching and learning to move students forward?

Make Resources Useful and Accessible

With student input, make resources accessible, and teach and practice how to use them. For example, make sure students know how to use word walls and how to choose "just right" books from the classroom library. Otherwise, these potentially useful resources become educational artifacts rather than sources and supports for learning.

This is part of a name word wall in a kindergarten classroom.

If you want your students to be independent, organize your space with that in mind. Word walls, especially helpful in the early grades for highlighting frequently used words and students' names, are easiest for students to use when they can reach them. Classmates' names are an easy way for most students to begin to learn letters and sounds because they have a known reference readily available. Talk about the special features of words as you post them and demonstrate how and why to use the word wall as a reading/writing tool.

Make sure procedures for getting more writing paper, sharpening pencils, using the bathroom, working with a peer, and so on are specific, clear, and easy for students to manage on their own.

Make Practice and Independent Work Worthwhile

Ensure that the work the rest of the students are doing while you are holding a conference or working with a small group is worthwhile and that it contributes to students' knowledge and growing independence. Also be sure that you have a way to evaluate the work students have done. If students are applying skills and strategies that you have taught them, independent work can be productive and valuable for moving their learning forward.

For example, after I've worked with a guided reading group, I keep the subsequent independent work focused on reading, not on activities *about* reading. The first assignment is always additional reading related to the reading they just did: rereading with a partner to practice fluency or reading the next chapter and briefly responding in writing to a question or two (which lets me know whether or not the student understood what he or she read).

Avoid the pitfall of wasting time on busywork—purposeless coloring, centers without meaningful activities, worksheets, and activities we never evaluate. What we ask students to do must be worth their time and ours and contribute to their growing literacy. Students must also be able to do their work without our help (or, in the case of homework, their parents' help). Students need to have received sufficient instruction, practice, and guidance so that they can work independently.

Place Responsibility on the Students

When I have trouble hearing the students in a small group because the noise level in the classroom is too loud, I stop and say something like, *I'm having a great deal of difficulty working with my group. Can someone tell me what the problem is?* And after someone does I might add, *What can you do to solve this problem?* I let students know that it is their job to manage their own behavior so everyone can get their work done.

In placing responsibility on students, I employ the Optimal Learning Model—demonstrating, explaining, collaborating on shared experiences, leading scaffolded conversations, charting criteria and expectations—for exactly what I expect students to do. I ask: *What is it I expect you to do?* I have students say back to me what the expectations for the task are. If they cannot, I know more demonstrations and explanations are necessary before students are sent off to work with minimal guidance. See Management Tips below.

One sure way to tell how well students are doing with self-management is what happens when they have a substitute teacher. If students have assumed responsibility for their behavior, the classroom operates as if the teacher were present. When things go badly, it's often a sign that the classroom discipline is maintained on the basis of teacher rewards and punishments.

TIPS FOR SELF-MANAGEMENT

- Make procedures and tasks explicit, clear, and easy to follow.
- Provide resources to support students' efforts. (Some examples include appropriate literature, peers, student spelling dictionaries.)
- Demonstrate and explain exactly the how and why of what you expect students to do. (Goals must be clear to our students and us.)
- Provide necessary supports and resources so students have the "know-how" and confidence to succeed.
- Assess to ensure students understand the expectations for the task.
- If students are unclear, demonstrate further, have them practice some more, and assess again.

continues

TIPS FOR SELF-MANAGEMENT, *continued*

- Provide lots of opportunity for talk ("turn-and-talk," small-group discussions, responsive questioning).

- Move at a steady pace. Stop while engagement is still high.

- Take a few minutes *before* students begin a task to be completed independently to meet with those few learners who still need support. (See photo, p. 93.)

- Gradually release responsibility to students to assume management responsibilities.

- If you need help, apprentice yourself to a teacher with excellent classroom management skills.

Teach Students to **Self-Monitor and Self-Evaluate**

Third graders are self-directing and self-monitoring while reading and writing nonfiction.

The more students can do for themselves, the less we have to do for them and the better off they and we are. It's a win-win situation. Structure all work so that students, as much as possible, can check, monitor, and direct their own learning. Build in assessment every step of the way. Check for understanding before, during, and after instruction (see Chapter 5). Teaching students to edit their written work is an excellent example of putting that self-monitoring into practice. The table on page 103, Self-Directed Learners, details the characteristics of students who are working as independent learners.

The ultimate purpose of evaluation is to:

- Improve teaching and learning.

- Enable students to self-evaluate.

Worthwhile student self-assessment depends on excellent teaching. Use the Optimal Learning Model to show students how to evaluate their own work. Self-assessment without student know-how is a waste of time. With effective self-assessment, students recognize the strengths and weaknesses of their work as well as where and how to make improvements and corrections, and they can do so independently.

One of the major reasons many students do not do better on high-stakes writing tests is that they have become dependent on us teachers to tell them when they need to check their spelling, revise, or reorganize. We have disabled them with all the help we provide.

SELF-DIRECTED LEARNERS

- Are intentional in their actions
- Appropriately manage their own behaviors
- Manage time effectively
- Problem solve and apply appropriate strategies
- Are aware of what they know and don't know
- Know how and when to seek help
- Know what next steps are necessary to take and how to take them
- Seek feedback from others and thoughtfully act upon that feedback
- Self-monitor, self-correct, and self-regulate
- Continue to learn on their own
- Reflect on their learning and actions
- Effectively self-evaluate
- Revise and modify their thoughts and actions
- Initiate and plan new action
- Adjust work to improve quality

(Adapted from Costa and Kallick, 2004).

Teach Self-Checking

Even young children can check their own work if we teach them how and provide the necessary support and expectations. For example, when doing "cut-up sentences" with kindergartners and first graders, I project my reassembled words on a screen so students can see what words are

Students of all ages can be taught to take responsibility for editing their work.

selected and in what sequence. When I ask students to do a closed sort or to "bring down a word" or to put their words in order, I ask, "Are you right? How did you know that? How can you check yourself?" When young students try to figure out a "mystery message" by deciphering words, letters, and sounds, I always ask, "How did you know that? How did you figure that out?" I am encouraging them to think about how they know. At first students say, "I just knew that." But with continued scaffolding ("I bet you knew that from a book," or "Did you see it on the word wall?" or "Did you think about the sounds those letters make together?") they eventually get good at saying how they knew.

We need to be relentless in not doing for students what they can figure out for themselves. Of course, we first need to have applied the Optimal Learning Model so students know how to check their own work. But then we can make them accountable for editing their writing; figuring out new words; making sure they have followed procedures, a rubric, directions; and so on.

We need to ask, *What can you do to help yourself?* Too often we teachers play the role of rescuer, which fosters dependency.

Expect Basic Conventions to Be Correct

Terri Thompson, an exemplary first-grade teacher in Westminster, Colorado, has negotiated with her first graders. They know she will not read their writing until they have incorporated the agreed on conventions: "No periods, no commas, no service." Even young students are capable of applying some conventions and spelling a small core of words correctly in their daily writing by accessing resources to check themselves. Terri notes:

I have seen a vast improvement because I don't overhelp. I kindly give the paper back to the student, and the missing conventions appear. Of course, the kids have caught on, and now correct conventions appear before they come up with their paper. What a time saver!

Key to having students take responsibility for conventions is having them write and publish for audiences and purposes that matter to them, showing how conventions are used through demonstration writing and shared writing, and providing lots of opportunities for guided practice and conferences before expecting students to use conventions independently.

Teach Students How to Take Over Goal Setting

Teach your students how to set their own reading and writing goals. For example, in a reading conference, ask students to name their strengths as a reader and what they need to work on. Being able to do this is very sophisticated. Students will first need a great deal of guidance and practice, but the payoff is huge.

Third-grade teacher Elizabeth Kappler comments:

This was one of my biggest "aha" moments after your last visit. I've now become much more specific about my feedback to students. I've been writing down the smart thinking and strategies students use when we confer and even when meeting with a child during a reading group. I've found students start to use the same language after I've modeled it this way. They'll say, "I did a good job of self-correcting there," or, "I read that part with expression."

I've also been surprised by the number of students who cannot tell me what they do well as a reader. I realized that I can't expect them to take control for their own goal setting and learning if they don't know what they're aiming for. Making goal setting an integral part of my reading program has helped me see this.

Teach Students How to Self-Direct Small, Collaborative Groups

When I teach students how to have meaningful literature conversations (see *Conversations*, Routman, 2000), I also teach them how to manage their groups. A number of heterogeneous groups of students (usually six or seven groups of four students each) simultaneously conduct their own group discussions. I am free either to join one group (as a supportive participant, coach, or demonstrator) or to move from group to group and take notes on what I observe and give feedback later. The goal is for students to handle their own management problems and comprehend and converse at a high level. Once students become proficient working together, these small interactive groups can be used for work in math, social studies, science, or any subject area.

In a third-grade classroom in which students did not get along well and there were continual instances of off-task behavior, group dynamics and individual behavior greatly improved once students successfully implemented self-directed literature conversations. Learning how to self-manage behavior and think-through a text together transferred across the classroom and across the curriculum. Students successfully applied the same group structure to read and think through—and sometimes summarize—a news article, a chapter in a content area text, math problems.

Here's a brief outline for how to introduce self-directed conversations or any self-directed small-group work at any grade level:

- Demonstrate/explain the purpose and procedures.

- Conduct a "fishbowl" demonstration. Lead and facilitate a small-group discussion as the remaining students observe. Have the observers take notes to ensure participation and accountability.

- Discuss the role of facilitator: what he or she does, the fact that facilitators are first chosen by the teacher, then by the kids in the group.
- Investigate the role of a group member as a shared writing
- Evaluate orally and in writing what makes a worthwhile conversation (first as a shared and guided discussion, then using shared writing and guided practice, and then independently). The evaluation serves as a useful debriefing to improve quality after every self-directed conversation or small-group work.

These specific expectations for self-directed, small-group work lead to ongoing checking, improving, and self-monitoring.

Eventually, with lots of guidance and practice, students can effectively evaluate on their own how well the groups have worked and set goals for improving both procedures and topics of conversation. Third-grade teacher Elizabeth Kappler comments, "The debriefing after a fishbowl demonstration is a great strategy and something I've been able to apply to other contexts."

Prepare Students for Testing

Fourth-grade teachers in Colorado taught students how to evaluate and improve their writing using district rubrics and the state writing test rubric. The teachers' original purpose was *How do we find the time in the day to confer with individual students to help them improve their writing?* A secondary purpose was for students to be able to transfer their writing abilities to the high-stakes writing test. Students learned not only how to score and evaluate their work the way a teacher and commercial scorer would, but also how to determine what improvements were needed in their writing samples and how to make them. More important, students finally assumed responsibility for evaluating and directing all of their own writing. The result was more competent students, better writers, higher test scores, and less work for their teachers.

Here's what happened. After three years spent focusing on writing in schoolwide residencies, we were still disappointed with test scores. Teachers struggled to find time to confer individually with students about their writing. While some teachers were seeing better student writing in their classrooms, what most students were accomplishing on tests did not reflect this improvement. I suggested that the problem was student dependency. Students were still expecting teachers to assume responsibility for improving their writing.

Following the Optimal Learning Model, Cami Kostecki and Kaylene Jenkins set out to change the situation. First they looked at the district rubric with their students for the stated purpose of having students look at their own writing and make it better. Applying "teach it first, label it later," they never mentioned testing until after students had been immersed in competent demonstrations, small-group work, lots of practice, and guided feedback.

Applying responsive teaching, Cami and Kaylene asked their students, "What is a rubric?" Few knew. Examining and discussing the district rubric, students came to understand it as a way to look at their writing to see what they were already doing well and what they needed to do to make their writing better. One student said, "A rubric could help me set goals for my writing." With teacher guidance, the students, over several days, took all the components on the district rubric—content, organization, word choice, and so on—one at a time, and converted the expectations into language they could understand. Students worked in small groups so all voices were heard. Then they came together as a whole group to negotiate final versions for each category, presented as "I will" statements. (See page 108.)

> "*Examining and discussing the district rubric, students came to understand it as a way to look at their writing to see what they were already doing well and what they needed to do to make their writing better.*"

Exchanging several writing samples (without names) from each other's classrooms, Cami and Kaylene modeled how to use the newly created rubric to score a paper and set goals for improvement. Each of them:

- Demonstrated by talking out loud, rereading the paper, and explaining her thinking as she evaluated the piece.
- Invited students to participate in the scoring process.
- Guided small groups of four as they met to score a different writing sample (all students worked on the same one) and then came together as a class to discuss their results.
- Provided additional practice on another student writing sample ("Pretend you're the teacher and this is your student's paper. Make a list of what you'd tell this student to work on to be a better writer.") The class then came together to decide the three or four most important things that needed to be done to improve this student's writing.
- Expected students to score their own midyear, district-required writing sample, list what they had done well, and set individual goals to improve their writing.
- Compared her scores on the midyear samples with the students' scores.

FOURTH-GRADE PERSONAL NARRATIVE—
STUDENT EXPECTATIONS (RUBRIC)

Name _____ Title _____ Date _____

I will . . .

CONTENT & IDEAS

____ write a story about an event that happened
____ follow the prompt **completely**
____ use details that are interesting, important, and on target
____ use enough details to completely tell my story (it is a "just right" length)
____ show, not tell (create a picture in my reader's mind)
____ use sensory details (see, hear, taste, feel, smell)

ORGANIZATION

____ use a good lead
____ have a middle that supports my topic
____ use an ending (close the story)
____ write my ideas in order (don't skip around)
____ use transition words or phrases to help make my story make sense (*while, after that, in the meantime*) if they are needed
____ write my thoughts and ideas into paragraphs
____ choose a catchy title that fits the whole story

CONVENTIONS

____ use correct spelling (K–4 "no excuse" words)
____ use correct punctuation (' . : ! , ? " " —)
____ use correct grammar
____ use capitals when needed (no random capitals)
____ use the same format throughout my story
____ write neatly

VOICE

____ use words, phrases, and sentences that show my own personality (it sounds like me)
____ use words or sentences to tell how I feel
____ make my story sound like a natural conversation I would have
____ use voice that is lively and interesting (BIG letters, underlined, **bold**, !!!, etc . . .)

WORD CHOICE

____ use describing words (juicy adjectives and adverbs)
____ use specific words (school, Arapahoe Ridge)
____ use similes so I can paint a picture in my reader's mind (use *like* or *as* to compare things)
____ use strong, powerful verbs (show action)

SENTENCE FLUENCY

____ write in complete sentences
____ use short and long sentences (short: I love my black dog, I love my furry cat.) (long: I love my black dog, and my furry cat.)
____ vary my words at the beginning of my sentences
____ use dialogue
____ make my sentences *FLOW* with each other

Cami and Kaylene each needed to meet with only four students to discuss scoring discrepancies, and all of these were struggling students who still had difficulty assessing themselves.

As a result of reworking the rubric and practicing writing on demand throughout the year—quick-writes, prompts, remembrances, and learning experiences—almost all the students were capable of scoring their own papers and setting appropriate goals independently. Now students were ready to hear and understand when Cami and Kaylene said: *Kids, state testing is coming up in a few weeks. Your writing will be judged with a rubric, just like the one we made. Now you know exactly how you will be scored and how you can improve your writing to make it your best work.*

Just before their students took the state tests, both teachers emphasized "do your best for yourself, your family, and your school." Students took the test confidently and produced high-quality writing, despite a fanciful and awkward prompt. Their understanding of the writing standard-setting process they had undertaken comes through in their comments. (See the students' quotes below). Cami and Kaylene were so impressed with their students' performance that they actively promoted schoolwide conversations in order to get this kind of self-assessment rolling in the early grades. This process is now implemented schoolwide at the beginning of the school year

> *"I felt very happy when my class rewrote the fourth grade rubric. I can't wait to write another story with all these tips."*
> —CALVIN P.

> *"Rewriting the fourth grade rubric has helped me understand what I have to include in my stories."*
> —ALYSSA T.

> *"...It made me feel a whole lot better as a writer."*
> —KYLE M.

> *"...When we were done a shock went through me. It told me, 'This is what I have to do.' It really improved my writing."*
> —KYLE G.

> *"...I noticed what I needed to work on and I memorized the whole rubric. I understood it better because it was in my words."*
> —TARA K.

Rewriting our rubric was quite an experience. Now that I've gone through this process, though, I don't like to think of it as a rubric, but as a goal sheet for my fourth grade writing.
    —Sabrina W.

"...It helped me improve my writing because when I do CSASP (the state test) if I have to write a story...BAM! Nothing can stop me."
    —Branden S.

What can you do in your own school to create a "Bam! Nothing can stop me!" confidence in your learners? Start small. Select a single, manageable project with your students and/or with your grade-level colleagues that would increase students' ownership of their learning. Rewrite a rubric together or take the Optimal Learning Model on the inside front cover of this book and use it as a tool for change. Provide lots of collaborative practice time. Work thoughtfully. You and your students may be transformed.

Independent, **Self-Directed** Learners

> " *It is vital to the culture of the school and the integrity of the all-school coaching model that we keep all conversations about what we see and/or hear during visits professional. That itself has the capacity to make or break the experience.*"
>
> —TRENA SPIERS, PRINCIPAL OF A K–5 ELEMENTARY SCHOOL

CHAPTER 7

Put **Schoolwide Coaching** into Practice

I HAD JUST FINISHED THE BEST WEEK I'd ever experienced in ten years of doing school residencies, a week spent coaching teachers I had previously worked with in a school where I had bonded closely with the staff.

It was a typical school where reading scores had remained flat for years. We had spent two years working on improving reading practices (with excellent and sustained student gains in reading achievement on various measures, including state tests) as well as enjoyment. We had then moved to focus on writing for two years (with slower gains in achievement across all the grades). This fifth year, my plan was to coach strong teachers (who by their own admission felt ready) so they could go on and coach others. The goal was that even when I no longer returned, the school would be self-sustaining because of its "each one teach one" culture.

I knew this was a tall order given the school had a young, new, first-time principal. There were also a few new teachers, some brand new to the profession; two were district transfers. Still, I felt undaunted. My heart swelled with pride as I coached teachers in their classrooms. I witnessed some of the finest teaching I had ever seen, confirmed by observing teachers from adjacent grade levels and by

> *Applying the learning model to coaching may seem simple, but when I was caught up in the day-to-day survival of coaching, I lost sight of how to give a teacher the support he needed without taking over for him. When I slowed down and added the shared piece ('We do it'), I was far more successful."*
>
> —DARCY BALLENTINE, FIRST-YEAR LITERACY COACH

several administrators also in attendance. We noted smart application of the Optimal Learning Model, responsive teaching, embedded assessment, full student engagement, accommodations for special needs learners, student self-assessment, and most importantly, joy in teaching and learning.

After each coaching session, during which I had taken notes on the entire lesson—what was taught, what was said—I gave each teacher detailed feedback. First I reported the strengths of what she or he had done and then gave some gently worded suggestions, along with a copy of my notes. (With the teacher's permission, people who had observed the lesson also sat in on the debriefing session.)

As is customary in my residencies, the whole staff met after school each day to talk about teaching and learning and share their experiences—what they were trying out, thinking about, and questioning. Our main goal for this week was to come up with a plan to put an all-school coaching program into place, so that the teachers I had coached would be able to coach others. (Any teachers who wanted to be part of the coaching program could be.) Some teachers worried that they would feel evaluated or that "everyone will know what I don't know," but we appeared to work through those feelings of discomfort. This was a staff that collaborated with and trusted one another. Teachers said they felt ready, at a minimum, to observe one another at and across grade levels, beginning by focusing on their strengths. I left the school feeling confident all would fall into place.

On my return visit a year later, nothing much had happened. For the most part, teachers did not "step up to the plate" and coach one another. I was forced to take a critical look at this all-school coaching failure.

Remember, It's **Harder** Than It Looks

All of us learn almost everything we know through demonstration, practice, and coaching. Rightfully, therefore, coaching has become a popular educational practice, but how well it works is open to debate. Because coaching can impact learning so powerfully, we need to examine the potential, the pitfalls, and the possibilities.

Here's what I've observed in the work I've done across the country. Literacy coaches are in place in many schools—meeting with teachers, assessing their needs, providing resources, presenting demonstration lessons, and observing teachers present follow-up lessons. In some cases, the coaches are highly knowledgeable about effective instruction and working with teachers. In too many cases, however, coaches have limited skills and are "trained," often hurriedly, to work with their peers. Some of these coaches are mediocre teachers, pulled from their classroom because the district has instituted a coaching program. Even when coaches are knowledgeable about literacy, they often fall short in effecting long-term, meaningful change. I have rarely seen coaching in a school or district that, after a few years, impacts student achievement. This is the bottom line: *Are the students learning more? How do you know?* Without such evidence, schoolwide and districtwide coaching is essentially a waste of time.

Rethink Your Coaching Plan

I was humbled by my own coaching failure, because my job as a mentor teacher is primarily that of a coach. I demonstrate, cheerlead, co-teach, problem solve with teachers, scaffold, hand-hold, share research and resources, and more. One to one with teachers I have had many successes, but moving a whole school to implement successful coaching is more difficult and has caused me to do some hard rethinking. I have come to see that typical halftime, well-intentioned literacy coaches, tiptoeing around teachers' feelings out of genuine respect for these colleagues, can't make enough of a difference to impact a whole school. Every teacher has to be part of an effective coaching program if the entire school is to move toward and maintain higher student achievement.

In carefully analyzing what had gone wrong and why teachers had not taken a leadership role in coaching one another, I realized several things. First of all, when debriefing the teachers I had coached, rather than beginning, *What went well in the lesson?*, I took over and did all the talking. I read from my notes: *Here's what I noticed that you did well,* or, *These were strengths I observed.* I took away any opportunity for the teachers to celebrate their successes, self-reflect, self-evaluate, and, with guidance, set new goals and work toward independence. Rather than embrace responsive teaching, which encourages the learner to be reflective and responsible, I fell back on telling. In taking over and doing most of the talking, I effectively shut down dialogue as well as opportunities for guided problem solving and greater teacher awareness of how the lesson had gone, including suggested changes for improvement.

Nor had I provided a structure or framework for teachers to follow. We had talked about what effective coaching might look like, but we had no written guidelines. I had also failed to follow the Optimal Learning Model and provide many shared experiences *before* expecting teachers to

> *"I have come to see that typical halftime, well-intentioned literacy coaches, tiptoeing around teachers' feelings out of genuine respect for these colleagues, can't make enough of a difference to impact a whole school."*

A valuable scenario is to coach an experienced teacher in a guided reading group so she can coach others.

attempt schoolwide coaching on their own. I cannot emphasize enough how crucial the "We do it" phase is for success—in any learning endeavor.

Consider the coaching efforts in your school, whether that means taking into account the role of the literacy coach or the manner in which teachers support, mentor, and coach each other. What's working well? What are the challenges? What changes might be considered to make coaching a positive schoolwide journey that could impact school achievement? Until we are all honest with one another about the pitfalls of coaching, we won't gain much ground. It's got to be carried out in a way where all teachers feel respected and are given immediate opportunities to shape the professional conversation. A "We Can Do It!" spirit needs to fill the air.

Put a **Whole-School Plan** into Practice

I recently tried out my revised thinking about schoolwide coaching at another school where, for three successive years, I had been conducting weekly residencies to improve the teaching of reading. As a result of strong principal leadership, weekly professional conversations, and application in the classroom of what was demonstrated in the residency, our success was being verified in classroom assessments, periodic district assessments, and much improved state test scores in reading (scores had gone from 53 percent proficiency to 80 percent proficiency and been maintained, to date, for three years). We also saw greater reading comprehension (as evaluated in reading conferences and small-group work) and most important, experienced a sense of joy in teaching and learning.

The principal requested we focus the upcoming residency on writing. When I suggested that we focus instead on one more year teaching reading with an emphasis on getting a schoolwide coaching model into place, she concurred. I was concerned that without such a coaching program, the school would be unable to maintain its high reading achievement. The student body was primarily low income, there was a large English language learner population, and there were several new teachers who lacked experience and know-how in teaching reading. I knew from experience that the whole school needed to be "on board" to have high achievement schoolwide. The model we tried (and continue to modify) has proved effective.

Make Sure Coaching Is Nonthreatening, Nonevaluative, and Focused on Student Learning

The biggest challenge in setting up an effective coaching program is making teachers feel valued and confident enough to take risks and, at the same time, not feel that they are being judged by anyone other than themselves. Confidentiality is also a big issue. Teachers have to know the coach is not talking about anyone except in supportive ways; trust is essential for coaching to succeed. Whoever is being coached has to feel the process is inclusive, fair, and open. As one teacher put it, "I am coachable only when I'm part of the conversation."

Another weighty issue is that the coaching has to be rigorous—it has to establish high standards for effective teaching and produce evidence that students are learning. It is not enough for teachers (and coaches) to become more knowledgeable about research and literacy practices. That knowledge and coaching support has to translate into demonstrable gains in student achievement, as evidenced in daily work samples, conferences, anecdotal notes, student self-evaluations, district assessments, and state testing.

Recognizing that previously I had not provided a framework for what as coaches and teachers we would be aiming for and talking about, I created the common goals, language, and expectations in the chart below, Looking at Your Teaching. This form gave everyone the same expectations for planning, teaching, and evaluating and also made it possible for peers to talk about a lesson using the questions provided (which are seen as neutral) rather than making up their own questions (which peers might perceive as evaluative). You can download this form from the *Teaching Essentials* site on www.regieroutman.com.

LOOKING AT YOUR TEACHING

Planning Ahead:

- What is the purpose of your lesson and what are the goals? How relevant are they to students' needs and interests as well as to "best" literacy practices?

- How will you ensure students know and understand the lesson purpose and goals?

- What stage of the Optimal Learning Model are you in and why? (How much demonstrating and support do students need?)

- What do you want students to be able to do?

- What resources and teaching methods will you use?

- How will you accommodate, support, and differentiate instruction for struggling learners, English language learners, and gifted students?

- How will you know students have succeeded?

Teaching and Learning:

- Is the teaching "responsive teaching" or "telling teaching"?

- Who is doing most of the work?

- What opportunities do students have to talk and interact?

- How does the pacing of your lesson impact student engagement?

- How is assessment embedded into the lesson?

- How is instruction adjusted according to students' responses?

- How are you providing time for guided and independent practice?

- How are students' efforts and achievements celebrated?

Evaluating:

- What went well? (Name all you did that contributes to students' success.)

- Is there anything you think you might have done differently?

- How independent are the students in problem solving, finding and using resources, self-monitoring, self-evaluation?

- What have students learned? What is your evidence?

- How can you provide additional support for students who need it most?

- How are students evaluating their own learning and setting new goals?

- Are students doing their best work or are they satisfied to do mediocre work?

- What are your next steps and why?

Teachers like using the "Looking at Your Teaching" form because it helps them thoughtfully plan, teach, and evaluate their lessons. A first-year literacy coach commented:

> *The "Looking at Your Teaching" form has helped a lot in keeping things positive and allowing teachers to be more reflective. You're absolutely right about the pressure being off the people coming to watch, since the ones getting observed know what's expected before people come and talk with them. People seem excited about the whole process. (Ballentine, 2007)*

The questions on the form help provide a clear picture of what effective teaching comprises as well as the language to use when talking about the lesson. Just as important, they put the responsibility for the lesson on the teacher, where it belongs. It is now the teacher who has been coached who talks about what has gone well, what changes need to be made, what else might have been tried, and so on. Once the teacher names all that has gone well, then one or more of the observing teachers (trying out the role of coach) add their positive comments. These comments are specific, such as:

- *The way you used turn-and-talk gave everyone a chance to be heard. Then you called on the partner to respond, which was a great assessment to see who's listening.*

- *When you began your shared writing, you said, "What's an interesting first sentence to let our readers know what this is all about?" You didn't just say, "Who has a first sentence?"*

- *When you introduced the book to your small guided reading group, you said, "Here's a tricky part: 'Away goes little rabbit.' Practice it." Then you checked each student one by one and told a few, "Read it again." You made sure students were secure with that line before expecting them to read on their own.*

Only after the teacher who is being coached talks about possible ways the lesson might have been stronger (*Is there anything you think you might have done differently?*) does the coach weigh in with comments. Even then, these comments are based on notes taken during the lesson: *You said such-and-so. Say more about that. When Jason said such-and-such, you said thus-and-so. Talk about your thinking there.* Only when the teacher has said everything she has to say does the coach chime in with, *Here's something I was thinking you might have tried here . . .* (Even when the teacher who is being coached is unaware a lesson has gone badly, beginning with positive feedback makes it more likely the teacher will be receptive to suggestions.)

Because the teacher-learners have taken responsibility for evaluating their own teaching and have first received genuine positive feedback, an honest suggestion at the end is not devastating. Even when teachers have been disappointed with how a lesson has gone, they are disappointed with themselves—not the coach—and strive to do better. This self-reflection and independence is exactly what we want for our students, too.

"Looking at Your Teaching" is also helpful as a peer observation guide for giving feedback to a fellow teacher. Just as the coach does, the observing teacher takes notes on exactly what the demonstrating teacher does and says, without judgment, and has the demonstrating teacher take over how the lesson has gone, naming and evaluating what she or he had done. Another benefit has been that principals have found the form useful for knowing what to look for and focus on in an effective lesson.

Add Shared Experiences to Any Coaching Instruction

I'm coaching a grade 5–6 teacher in her first informal reading conference.

When I observe coaches, even knowledgeable ones, most often the hand-holding—shared demonstration—is missing. Typically, a coach demonstrates a lesson for a teacher, the teacher observes and may take notes, the teacher and coach debrief the lesson, and the teacher plans and tries out a similar lesson. Not surprisingly, the lesson often doesn't go very well. The coach has moved from demonstration to independent practice without first providing the necessary support through "We do it" experiences. When coaches add this crucial shared piece, the results can be dramatic. In particular, because the teacher is now prepared and ready to teach (having had sufficient co-teaching and guided practice), she is more likely to be successful right from

THE OPTIMAL LEARNING MODEL

Teaching and Learning Contexts	Who Holds Book/Pen	Degree of Explicitness/Support
Celebration & Assessment Are Embedded		
Reading and Writing Aloud	**Teacher**/Student	**Demonstration**
Shared Reading and Writing Scaffolded Conversations	**Teacher**/Student	**Shared Demonstration**
gradual handover of responsibility		
Guided Reading Literature Conversations Reading/Writing Conferences	**Student**/Teacher	**Guided Practice**
Independent Reading/Writing	**Student**/Teacher	**Independent Practice**
Celebration & Assessment Are Embedded		

the start. As well, conversations about the lesson are more meaningful, and the gradual "handover" of responsibility puts the teacher in charge.

Whether in the role of coach or teacher, to be effective you will want to apply the Optimal Learning Model *before* coaching or being coached as below). Of course, it's a given that both the teacher and the coach are reliable—that they show up on time and are prepared.

If you are the coach, prepare yourself before you coach:

- *Demonstration*—Observe what an expert does coaching you as well as other teachers—planning, pacing, modeling, language used, content of lesson, responsiveness to students, resources, support provided, assessing, debriefing.
- *Shared demonstration*—Coach a teacher with an expert coach observing, giving you feedback, and co-coaching as needed. (You may need to have this experience several times.) Debrief together.
- *Guided practice*—Coach a teacher and then debrief with an expert who has also observed the coaching session. Have the expert give you feedback on your coaching after you name what went well and what else might have been done.
- *Independent practice*—Coach a teacher. Use "Looking at Your Teaching" or a similar form you create to talk about the lesson with the teacher and set new goals.

When there is no "expert coach" available, get together with the principal, assistant principal, or a teacher you admire and have one or more practice coaching sessions in a classroom. Give each other feedback before attempting the role of coach.

If you are the one being coached:

- *Demonstration*—Co-plan with the coach. Observe and take notes as the coach teaches and assesses your students. Debrief; ask questions.
- *Shared demonstration*—Co-plan and co-teach a similar lesson with the coach. (This stage may need to be repeated several times.)
- *Guided practice*—Teach a lesson with the expectation that the coach will "jump in" as needed. Name your strengths and what else might have been tried.
- *Independent practice*—Teach a lesson. Self-evaluate and set new goals.

Expand the Role of Principal to Co-Teacher and Support Teacher

Another big challenge has been how to coach principals to expand their role from evaluator to co-teacher and/or support teacher and to get both principals and teachers to see these two roles as distinct.

At first, and with good reason, teachers are nervous and untrusting, since their principal is their primary evaluator. But it is not necessary for principals to wear that hat every time they come into the room. Principals and teachers share a mutual interest, the progress of the students. When they work together for their students' success, they can often put a stop to measures that engender fear and destroy necessary collegial trust.

Once a principal demonstrates herself to be a coach who is there, on-site, to support a teacher's efforts any way they can, teachers come to welcome and trust that new role. I advise principals to set aside an hour a day during which they go into classrooms as a coach and to enter that time on their calendars as inviolate.

It is a given that principals must also be knowledgeable and have a strong knowledge of content. If you are a principal or literacy leader without such knowledge, apprentice yourself to a teacher or colleague who has it. Read professionally. Attend excellent literacy conferences with one or more of your teachers. Spend time in classrooms in which teachers are applying best literacy practices and getting results. Become an integral part of schoolwide professional conversations as an equal participant and learner.

When I support principals who are moving into this new position, I apply the Optimal Learning Model just as I do with teachers. Together we go into a classroom and I demonstrate how to be supportive. Next we co-coach. Then I provide guidance as the principal gradually takes over. Here are some key factors for a principal-as-coach to incorporate:

- Take a more relaxed stance.
- Look for what's going well and comment on it.
- Ask what support the teacher needs. *How can I help you?*
- Listen carefully and be nonjudgmental.
- Use respectful language and conversation (not interrogation).
- Sit down next to the teacher and students and join in the lesson.
- Have a-go at co-teaching.
- Take notes on things to celebrate—for example, students' strengths as readers and writers.

- Take notes on what can be viewed as schoolwide issues and, without blame, bring these to a staff meeting for problem solving and moving forward. (Typical issues that have surfaced include needing better legibility and spelling in daily written work, supporting struggling readers and writers, understanding and applying the Optimal Learning Model, making the classroom library accessible to all students, appropriate use of "centers.")
- Arrange opportunities for teachers to visit peers' classrooms.
- Set up regularly scheduled times for grade-level staff to collaborate, problem solve, and share.

Provide Time, Support, and Trust for All-School Coaching

Understandably, teachers complain they don't have the time to be coaches. They are caught up in the day-to-day and are reluctant to use any of their limited time to hold coaching sessions, make lesson plans for the substitute covering their class, and debrief the person they are coaching.

The only way around these issues is to value all-school coaching, make it a priority, and enlist the support of the principal to make it a reality. Schools do make it a priority when they come to know that attaining and maintaining high achievement depends on all teachers being knowledgeable and effective, not just having a "star" teacher here and there. More than that, there must be a core group who keep things going. Teachers, coaches, and principals leave; new teachers and administrators come on board. All-school coaching helps ensure continuity of effective practices, adequate support, and sustained achievement.

Along with finding the time, another difficult element is creating a school culture in which teachers trust each other enough to say, "Come observe me and give me feedback." Here are some tips to effectively implement schoolwide coaching:

- Use your release time (when students go to music or physical education, for example) to go to another classroom to observe or coach.
- If you have a building literacy coach, have the coach take over teachers' classes so they can observe one another and work together. (At the school where Kathleen Poole is principal, the math coach will take a teacher's kids for math while the teacher goes next door and teaches or observes a grade-level partner. All three teachers debrief the lesson at lunch or at the end of the day.)

- Be flexible. Conduct observations as necessary rather than according to a rigid schedule. (Kathleen Poole says, "It's really based on learning what teachers need to know to address the particular issue they're struggling with, whether that need is identified by themselves or from an evaluator or an assessment.")

- Build in time to debrief so teachers aren't expected to do so before school or after school or during their planning time.

- Keep the atmosphere positive. Do what you can to build trusting relationships.

- The end result of coaching must be student progress and achievement. Constantly monitor and adjust to make that goal a reality.

Mary Yuhas, a teacher at Kathleen Poole's school, also advises that we work to keep our conversations primarily on kids and what they know instead of on what the teacher did or didn't do: "Focusing first on what the students say and do and then talking about what the teacher did to elicit those responses takes a lot of the 'evaluative feel' away from the conversation."

Still, many teachers have anxiety and fear about having their colleagues visit their classrooms. ("What if everyone finds out I'm not that good?") To address that issue, principal Trena Spiers uses the Optimal Learning Model to provide support for her staff and to frontload teachers much as we do our students. She, the literacy coach, and the student achievement coach set the structure and first walk the staff through the

process. They model the "pre-planning" discussion and the debriefing between two volunteer grade levels (fourth grade visited third) so the whole staff can hear the language and see the process *before* they participate themselves. In addition, each group of teachers visiting another classroom is accompanied by an administrator or coach during the visit and debrief, which serves various purposes. First, it fosters the role of "principal as a coach"; second, it provides the support teachers need; third, it sends the message to the community that student achievement is important to everyone, and what happens on a daily basis matters.

Meet the Challenge:
The Effort Is Worth It

All-school coaching is about effective instructional collaboration:

- The focus needs to be on instruction and assessment.
- Teachers must concentrate on teaching and supporting one another.
- There must be frequent, precise, intentional talk about teaching and learning.
- Instruction must be adjusted and improved on the basis of continuous, collective analysis of student work.

After-school professional conversations enhance the coaching and teaching done during the school day.

Whole-school coaching—necessary for all-school high achievement—is really about partnering with colleagues. While a whole-school coaching partnership is a challenge to implement, the payoff is huge: increased collaboration, more effective teaching, higher student achievement. These benefits help lessen the pressure of being observed and remind teachers and administrators of the larger purposes: celebrating successes, getting new ideas, refining teaching and assessing, and keeping the focus on the students.

The tricky part is that while coaches are not evaluators, they do need to support and guide teachers to become more effective instructors and assessors. When that happens, the result is increased student learning along with more confident, happier students and teachers. It doesn't get any better than that.

"What do you love to do? Make time for it."

CHAPTER 8

Live a **Full Life**

A DEAR COLLEAGUE ONCE TOLD ME she was on a mission to improve kids' lives in school. "I'm not on a mission," I told her. "I'm passionate about my work, but once I leave the building, I try to live my life."

When I teach in schools, I work from early morning through late afternoon. I am available throughout the day to students, teachers, and administrators. I devote my full energies to doing the best possible job I can do, but when I leave the school or district, I do not assume responsibility for the change that does or does not occur. First, I have been teaching long enough to know I don't have the power or the right to change anyone. Second, lasting change happens from within. My work, at best, is a catalyst. Third, I am a more interesting person if I have stories to tell that are not just about school.

While writing this book and developing the *Transforming Our Teaching* projects, I usually worked every day, beginning early each morning. But by early afternoon, I stopped. I would go out for a few hours—often with my husband Frank—for a walk, for a ride, to the park, for a meal, for a view of the mountains or lake, or just to sit in our garden. Other days, I met a friend, cooked a meal, made preserves, went to the farmers market, baked a fruit tart, sat quietly with a book, or planted flowers. I also continued to spend as much time as possible with my dad at the nursing home and, on occasion, took care

NOW
by Regie Routman

What do you love to do?
Make time for it.
Work will be there
Always constant
But
Love is fleeting
So is a sunrise
The bloom of an iris
A walk in the park
A child's laughter
Time with a friend

What do you love to do?
Go do it, savor it
Now

of our granddaughters. I would often work again for a short time in the evening, but keeping a few hours each day for living enabled me to keep some balance in my life. Without that balance, I could not maintain the high energy and commitment needed to do optimal work. As a dear colleague wrote me when I told him I was out in the garden after a long, wet, cold winter, "Keep taking those garden walks. Life needs its moments of quiet contemplation in order to be any life at all."

Let Yourself **Be Known**

"You will be able to do everything I do as a teacher. I don't do anything hard. Life is hard. We need to make teaching less stressful and more fun."

Let yourself be known as a reader, writer, thinker, person. The very first thing I do when I enter a classroom is tell stories—about my life, my family, what I like to do, what I'm reading. Without that personal connection, I can't teach the students very well. It's hard to learn from someone you don't trust.

I talk about my reading and writing, my husband Frank who is an artist, Norman the neighborhood cat who we have adopted, my disabled dad who lives close by in a nursing home, my granddaughters Katie and Brooke, all the things that are important to me. I gather the children close around me and invite them into my life as I hope they may invite me into theirs. I want them and the teachers to know I am just like them. I talk about (and show photos of) my family, what I am presently reading and writing, our move to Seattle, what I am struggling with. I say, "How many of you have moved to a new home or city? So you know it's not easy," and, "I love it when Katie and Brooke visit because all we do is play," and, "My dad lives close by in a nursing home, and we visit him often. How many of you are dealing with something hard in your life, too?"

Tell **Stories** with Relish

Stories are the way I bond with kids, both the life stories I tell and the stories I read. I choose stories that I know will engage them, and I pull out all the stops. I include lots of details, suspense, and excitement. These days I tell lots of stories about Norman, the outdoor, black, mangy, neighborhood cat that was foisted on us by the former owner of our house. Both Frank and I had an aversion to cats and had never touched one, but slowly, over several years, we fell in love with Norman (a she), who is now a silky, beautiful, mostly indoor cat that we adore. I tell and write about petting Norman for the first time, Frank feeding her expensive tuna fish, raccoons at our back door attracted by her cat food, getting an electric heating pad for her outdoor house, the night she had an all night walkabout, and how Norman now sleeps on our light-colored sofa. It is through stories that we make the human connections so necessary for building the trusting relationships that ground any learning community.

Simplify

Simplify and enjoy. I tell teachers, "You will be able to do everything I do as a teacher. I don't do anything hard. Life is hard. We need to make teaching less stressful and more fun." We need to find more enjoyment and eliminate, as much as we can, the hard parts. Some of the hard parts are unavoidable—district requirements, testing, new curriculum mandates, students who are challenging—but many of the hard parts are self-imposed—the amount of time we spend planning, the complexity of our projects, the length of reports we assign, the number of hours we stay after school.

I ask teachers when I am new to a school, "What time do you leave school each day?" For many it is after 6 p.m. "Do you have someone waiting for you at home? Even if you don't, get home at a decent hour. Pamper yourself. Spend more time with your family and loved ones. Staying later at school will not make you a better teacher."

Longer and more complex isn't necessarily better. Have students write more short pieces and reports. Have them do more reading instead of assigning lots of independent "seat work." Find ways to make things easier without sacrificing quality. Spend most of your planning time thinking, not marking papers or creating elaborate centers.

One of the things I love best in the summer is to make fruit pies and tarts. When the berries in the Northwest are luscious and the stone fruits are beautifully ripe, I create all kinds of delicious and gorgeous desserts. It's sheer fun for me to do it, partly because it's quick and easy. I no longer roll out a piecrust because it's time consuming. I make the dough in the food processor and immediately press it into the pie pan and partially prebake it. Friends often ask for my fruit tart recipe, which is not written down. Emailing a dear friend to support her first fruit tart effort, I wrote:

> *It's all a bit like good teaching, isn't it? You can follow a recipe up to a point, but for best results you have to adjust as you go along, pay close attention, get the feel of it all, think of your audience, use the best resources, and enjoy what you're doing.*

When a new Apple product was recently released, a reviewer writing in *The New York Times* said it had the qualities of all Apple products, "simplicity, intelligence and whimsy." I wrote those three words down and posted them above my desk. I frequently refer to them as a metaphor for how I want to live my life.

Have More **Fun**

The first fruit tart I made this summer—a strawberry, raspberry, and blueberry tart (delicious!), and strawberry jam I made a few weeks before. I always make small batches of jam when I'm working on a writing project.

One of the things I love best about being a grandparent is the amount of time I spend playing and being silly. When Katie and Brooke are at our house, I set aside everything and play with them. We play house, bake cookies, have a puppet show, sing songs, build a castle with blocks, make play dough, make up games, play cards, build a city with blankets and chairs, look at spiders, play dress-up, have tea parties, and on and on. No matter how much stress I've been under, that playtime and sheer silliness cures it, at least for a while.

Arranging flowers is another favorite pastime. I buy flowers, usually at our local market, as a soul staple. In the summer, I pick flowers from our garden or buy them at local farmer's markets. I love taking a bunch of flowers and arranging them just so, stem by stem—for color, height, texture, variety—and placing them in various containers in our kitchen and living room. Flowers always lift my spirits and give me a sense of peace and beauty.

I also love to cook. Mostly I cook for Frank, and together we enjoy creating menus and cooking for family and friends. I relish going through recipes and modifying them with my own personal touches, shopping at small markets for the freshest ingredients, trying out new dishes and not being afraid to fail, tasting everything to get the seasoning just right, and making and arranging the dishes so everything looks and tastes wonderful. Frank and I also love to set a beautiful table. We want our guests to feel fussed over and welcome. We never repeat what we've done and always have great fun playing around with how the table will look—choosing the colors we want; selecting and arranging dishes, glasses, napkins; adding dramatic or fanciful touches.

And of course I belong to a book club. A group of about twelve teachers meets monthly to discuss an agreed on book, a noteworthy non-fiction or fiction title. The book discussions are lively and interesting, but what I enjoy most is the laughter. These are teachers who have known each other for many years, and even when we are facing tough life issues, humor bubbles up to the surface at every meeting.

What is it that you most enjoy? Make time for it. That "playtime" will give you energy, enrich your life, and make you a more interesting person.

Rely on **Hope**

I am an optimistic person. I see possibilities everywhere, but I am also a realist. I know I can only do so much for a teacher or student or loved one. I have learned, however, that we teachers and administrators can be heroes without being heroic. To do what we did with Kathy, Owen, and the "dream" students in grade five (see pp. 6–10, 12–15, and 17–18), changing their lives forever because these students now view themselves differently, did not require heroic efforts. The efforts we made did not take more than any dedicated educator is capable of—unfailing belief in the capabilities of all students, holding high expectations, and providing the teaching, resources, and support they needed. None of us who worked with those students turned our lives upside down to ensure their success. We did work unfailingly hard during school hours, and we remained committed to the students over many years. Their successes enriched our lives without becoming our lives.

We are teaching in difficult times. With all the government regulations, the required curriculum and standards, the high-stakes testing, the politics and bureaucracy of education, and the challenges of our increasingly diverse student populations, it's easy to get discouraged. Remember this. One week, one semester, one year with an outstanding teacher can change a child's life forever. Rise above the distractions and regulations and naysayers. Focus on the children in front of you, and create genuine hope for their futures. They deserve the best of what you have to offer. They are counting on you.

You can do it.

Notes and **References**

Chapter 1

2   Epigraphs are from Katherine, a college-bound eighth grader and Monica Haynes, a fifth-grade teacher.

3   "Money, Not Race Is Fueling New Push to Bolster Schools," by Tamar Lewis and David M. Herszenhorn, *The New York Times,* June 30, 2007, p. A7.

4   Ada, Alma Flor, illustrated by Elivia Savadier. 2002. *I Love Saturdays y domingos.* New York: Atheneum.

6   Routman, Regie. 2003. *Reading Essentials: The Specifics You Need to Teach Reading Well.* Portsmouth, NH: Heinemann.

7   Ryan, Pam Muñoz, illustrated by Elivia Savadier. 2002. *When Marian Sang: The True Recital of Marian Anderson.* New York: Scholastic.

7   Dahl, Roald, illustrated by Quentin Blake. 2001. *The Magic Finger.* New York: Puffin Books.

8   *Educational Leadership,* Dec. 2004/Jan. 2005. "If I Said Something Wrong, I Was Afraid," by Douglas B. Reeves, pp. 72–74, citing E. H. Stefanakis, "Assessing Young Immigrant Students: Are We Finding Their Strengths?" *Harvard Education Newsletter,* 20 (3), p. 7.

12   Chambers, Veronica, illustrated by Julie Maren. 2005. *Celia Cruz, Queen of Salsa.* New York: Dial Books for Young Readers.

14   The pages and experiences are captured in this school-published volume: *Dreams: Listen to Our Stories.* 2007. Adams 12 Five Star Schools, Fifth Grade Students. Westminster, CO.

Chapter 2

16   Epigraphs are from Owen, a third grader, and AlexSandra, a fifth grader and once-shy English language learner.

17   Routman, Regie. 2005. *Writing Essentials: Raising Expectations and Results While Simplifying Teaching.* Portsmouth, NH: Heinemann.

26   Clay, Marie. 2002. "Hearing Sounds in Words" test.

26   Ellis, Marlene. 2006. Personal letter to me.

28   Giovanni, Nikki, illustrated by Bryan Collier. 2005. *Rosa.* Austin, TX: Holt.

28   Yoo, Paula, illustrated by Dom Lee. 2005. *Sixteen Years in Sixteen Seconds: The Sammy Lee Story.* New York: Lee & Low.

Chapter 3

32   Epigraphs are from from Barbara Stallings, principal in a K–5 Title 1 school and Jane Curry, grade 1–2 teacher in British Columbia.

35   Moffett, Cerylle A. 2000. "Sustaining Change: The Answers Are Blowing in the Wind." *Educational Leadership*, April 2000, p. 36.

40   Allington, Richard. Quote is from Susan Ohanian's website, www.susanohanian.org.

40   Herbert, Bob. 2005.[on Playwright Arthur Miller] "The Public Thinker." *The New York Times.* OP ED, February 14, 2005, p. A23.

47   Rosenthal, David. 2006. Quoted in *The New York Times,* October 2, 2006, p. C7.

Chapter 4

48   Epigraphs are from Sandra Garcia, teacher of English language learners and literacy coach, and literacy coach Nancy McLean.

52   Duke, Nell, Victoria Purcell-Gates, Leigh A. Hall, and Cathy Towers. "Authentic Literacy Activities for Developing Comprehension and Writing." *The Reading Teacher.* Dec/Jan 2006/2007, pp. 344–55.

58   The literacy coach is Nancy McLean. She made the remarks to me in an email June 16, 2007.

59   Essential Academic Learning Requirements (EALRs).

62   Routman, Regie. 2003. *Reading Essentials: The Specifics You Need to Teach Reading Well.* Portsmouth, NH: Heinemann.

65   Wiggins, Grant, and Jay McTighe from *Understanding by Design.* 1998, Alexandria, VA: ASCD, quoted in *Conversations* (2000) by Regie Routman, p. 26.

66   Hatkoff, Isabella, Craig Hatkoff, and Dr. Paula Kahumbu with photographs by Peter Greste. 2006. *Owen & Mzee: The True Story of a Remarkable Friendship.* New York: Scholastic.

66   Hatkoff, Isabella, Craig Hatkoff, and Dr. Paula Kahumbu with photographs by Peter Greste. 2007. *Owen & Mzee: The Language of Friendship.* New York: Scholastic Press.

67   Blachowicz, Camille L. Z., Peter J. L. Fisher, Donna Ogle, and Susan Watts-Taffe. 2006. "Vocabulary: Questions from the Classroom." *Reading Research Quarterly.* Oct/Nov/Dec 2006, pp. 524–37.

Chapter 5

70   Epigraphs are from Terri S. Thompson, a grade one teacher and Richard Allington, noted educator.

72   ...Reliance on "telling" is not beneficial to students' reading achievement: Barbara Taylor, Debra Peterson, P. David Pearson, and Michael Rodriquez. 2002. "Looking Inside Classrooms: Reflecting on 'How' As Well As 'What' in Effective Reading Instruction." *The Reading Teacher,* November, pp. 270–79.

73   ...Feedback includes the following qualities: Grant Wiggins, "Less Teaching, More Assessing." 2006. *Education Update.* 48.2, February, pp. 1, 2.

80   Real caution is needed here: National Association of Educational Progress (NAEP) Reading 2004; U.S. Department of Education. The Nation's Report Card.

80   ...No emphasis on reading help above grade 3 for a decade: Richard Allington, email May 23, 2007.

80   ...the pressure is so great and only a handful of states: Peterson, Paul E., and Frederick M. Hess. 2005. "Johnny Can Read...in Some States." *Education Next,* Summer 2005.

80   ...not a single state: "States Found Way to Vary Widely on Education" by Tamar Lewin, *The New York Times:* National Report, June 8, 2007, p. A 80.

80 …and only a couple of states: Richard Allington, email, July 2, 2007. The States are South Carolina and Louisiana.

81 Thommie Piercy, a former K–5 principal is the current pre-K–12 Supervisor of Reading in Carroll County, MD. She is also the author of *Compelling Conversations: Connecting Leadership to Student Achievement* (Denver: Advanced Learning Press and American Association of School Administrators, 2006). See *Reading Essentials*, p. 111, for description of school reading policy.

Chapter 6

87 Epigraphs are from Natalie, a struggling learner and Elizabeth Kappler, third-grade teacher.

103 Self-Directed Learners chart adapted from pp. 84–91 in *Assessment Strategies for Self-Directed Learning* by Arthur Costa and Bena Kallick. 2004. Thousand Oaks, CA: Corwin Press.

105 …when I teach students how to have meaningful literature conversations: see *Conversations*, Regie Routman. 2000. Portsmouth, NH: Heinemann.

Chapter 7

112 Epigraphs are from Darcy Ballentine, first-year literacy coach and from Trena Spiers, principal of K–5 elementary school.

118 Extract is from an email from Darcy Ballentine.

Chapter 8

130 "Simplicity, intelligence and whimsy": Review in *The New York Times*, by David Pogue.

Index